g-I𝔫a𝔯...

CATCH THE MANN

ay 10, 1791.

," replied Mallet
?" " Sir," faid
s mafter, " wha
o venture that
rror ; why fhoul

ARRIAGES.
ature for the pre
Marriages.
es a perfon young
er, be denied an
nder, either by de-
rtunes.
debilitated love
let them be dear
o bridewell.
ly fellow, full
old, rich maid,
endo, and let hi

e mill ; and if the
young, let her de
ghts.
ng, marries know-
anded in the hand

arries to the exclu
fortunes, let ther
ifence, and fuff

ermagant, let hi
and let him wear
und his waift for

l without fortune;
t friends, marry :
Nova-Scotia, being
ept that of propa-

his cook or kitchen
her coach-man or
condemned to the

part of t
ports, th
uneafinefs
rties.
n fat
ARC
s info
ply to
of the
concerni
ruler of
of their
great w
kno
w

verbal re-
in a flate of
liberties and pro-
tere his
ol
fhould
faith er
p ify
afu the
dy refta
the p of the
ifhe f they
cha thro'
, i WS-
fho nny
e al in
or a Newa-
ugh ertainly
th uch is in-
led other tive
ftimulates, muft induce him to found an alarm
when danger is at hand ; for the deftruction of
a *free prefs* will be the firft object with men determined to enflave their fellow-citizens. Su
terminations, however, will never
the people continue watchful of the
tentive to the proceedings of go
liberal patrions of the arts, " A
FREE-PRESS holds a diftinguifhed rank."

AN EPISODE IN
AMERICAN JOURNALISM

AN EPISODE IN
AMERICAN JOURNALISM

A HISTORY OF
DAVID FROTHINGHAM
AND HIS
Long Island Herald

Beatrice Diamond

Published for the Graduate Faculty,
C. W. Post College of Long Island University
by
KENNIKAT PRESS
Port Washington, N. Y.
1964

Published for the Graduate Faculty,
C. W. Post College of Long Island University by
Kennikat Press
Copyright © 1964 by C. W. Post College
ALL RIGHTS RESERVED
Library of Congress Catalog Card No. 64-15546
Manufactured in the United States of America

CONTENTS

v

INTRODUCTION

FROTHINGHAM'S *Long Island Herald* was edited
and published by David Frothingham at Sag
Harbor from May 10, 1791, to December 17,
1798. The *Herald* was the first newspaper published on Long Island and David Frothingham
was the first printer. Thus Frothingham and his
paper have a unique place in local history. This
study is planned to show that the *Herald*, a typical Republican* country press of the period, and
its editor and publisher, David Frothingham,
in some measure reflected and effected certain
political points of view in the United States
during the Federalist period while George Washington and John Adams were President.

In order for the newspaper and its printer to be
placed in a better perspective, the scope of this
study extends further in time than the life of the
newspaper and goes beyond the boundary of Sag
Harbor, Long Island. To set the scene for a better understanding of the problems and sentiments
that beset the new nation during the heated
Federalist-Anti-Federalist debate, sketches of
the history of Colonial America and Colonial
Long Island have been included. These are by

---

*This was a term preferred by those opposed to the Fed-
eralist philosophy of government.

no means comprehensive but are intended to serve as a background to emphasize the flavor and spirit of the period when there were vigorous differences of opinion involving national interests. Inasmuch as the *Herald* was printed at Sag Harbor the account of Long Island history is directed toward the eastern end of the Island with Sag Harbor as the focal point.

Since this study is chiefly concerned with a Republican newspaper which of necessity reflected a Republican point of view, it may appear that the material is biased or that an attempt is being made to downgrade the remarkable achievements of the great American statesmen of the time. Such is not the purpose. It is intended to present a dramatic controversy taken from the pages of the *Herald*, as well as the life of David Frothingham, its editor. Excerpts from materials of that era are presented as written, using such factual information as was available. In these documents spelling varies and the language sometimes seems strange. Insofar as possible, manuscripts have been copied verbatim and the original spellings have been followed without the use of "*sic*".

At this time respectful acknowledgement must be given to the many people who assisted the writer in the preparation of this work.

The many librarians who expended much time and effort in furnishing the author with the available materials deserve recognition and heartfelt thanks, particularly, Miss Florence Block and Mr. Leroy Provins at the Queensborough Public Library, Mr. Rufus Langhans at the Smithtown Library, Mr. Charles Morrell at the Long Island Historical Society, and Mrs. Amy O. Bassford at the Easthampton Free Library. Their interest in the subject under study provided the necessary encouragement needed for the long and continued research. We are further indebted to Mrs. Bassford of the Easthampton Free Library for her kind cooperation in providing the photostat of Vol. I, No. 1 of *Frothingham's Long Island Herald*.

The writer would like to express her gratitude to Mr. Richard N. Powdrell, formerly a member of the Faculty of the School of Library Science, Graduate Division, C. W. Post College of Long Island University, from whom the inspiration for the subject of this study originated.

To Professor E. Hugh Behymer, Professor Christine Gilbert, and Professor Paul Winckler of the School of Library Science, Graduate Division, C. W. Post College of Long Island University, the writer extends her sincere thanks and appreciation for the pleasant and tactful guidance in molding this study to its present form.

B. D.

Roslyn Heights, N. Y.

AN EPISODE IN
AMERICAN JOURNALISM

COLONIAL AMERICA

THE PERIOD, 1791-1799 was a crucial time in the history of the United States as an independent nation. It marked a period of recovery from the ravages of a long war for freedom and, at the same time, it marked the period of Federalist control of the national government. Strife and struggle among the political leaders of both the Federalist and Anti-Federalist parties characterized this era, as each fought to impose his own principles in establishing a strong government that would survive and earn the respect of its own people as well as of those in other countries.

In order to appreciate the enormity of the problems of the period, 1791-1799, it is necessary to review briefly some of the events of the Revolutionary period. Starting in 1765, when England passed the Stamp Act, regulating stamp duties to be placed on all publications and legal and business documents, the American colonists began protesting in earnest against unfair taxation and exploitation by England. A Stamp Act Congress which included delegates from most of the colonies met in order to bring pressure on England to correct the injustice of taxation without representation and to demand the right of trial by jury. They declared that the Stamp Act was an infringement on the rights and liberties of the colonies. The Act was repealed with the stipulation that it be understood that the colonies were subjects of England wherein supreme sovereign power resided, not only on matters of taxation but on all other legislation as well. And so the stage was set. On the one hand, England felt that her power was supreme and, in return for colonial protection, she had a right to use the colonies as a source of revenue. On the other hand, the colonists were becoming more and more bitter and defiant over continuing new taxes.

The tax on tea resulted in open rebellion in Boston in 1773. The tempers of the colonists rose higher as the British became more determined to assert their authority as a sovereign power. On April 19, 1775, the date of the Battle of Lexington and Concord, the Revolutionary War started.

In June, 1775, Bunker Hill, just across the Charles River from Boston, was the scene of another important battle at the beginning of the War. Until March, 1776, when Howe evacuated his troops from Boston, the British were concentrating on subduing the colonies in Massachusetts and Virginia.

The Declaration of Independence in 1776 announced to the British and to the rest of the world that the colonists were no longer fighting to establish their rights as such, but were now fighting for independence.

With Burgoyne's surrender to Gates at Saratoga in October, 1777 came the turning point of the War. It was then that France, who had been secretly helping the colonies with the intent of hurting England, entered into a treaty of alliance with the colonies. The object of this treaty was mutual aid between the colonies and France against their common enemy England. The colonists agreed to come to the aid of France if that country were to become embroiled in a war with England. France, in return, promised to assist the colonies in their present struggle against England by providing the necessary military and naval power required to achieve and maintain the sovereignty of the United States as an independent power not only in government but in commerce as well. The alliance of the French with the Americans supplied the colonists with the additional resources sorely needed to turn the tide against the British. The resulting strength of the Colonial Army provided them with the strategic advantage of dispersing the British to various battlefronts where they were forced to combat not only the rebellious colonists but the skilled French Army and Navy.

In 1781, General Greene took command for the colonies and gradually Cornwallis was forced to withdraw his British troops northward into a trap at Yorktown,Virginia. There, with the combined efforts of the French fleet of DeGrasse and the French and American armies of Washington and Rochambeau, Cornwallis surrendered in October, 1781. The treaty of peace was signed in Paris on September 3, 1783, the United States being represented by Benjamin Franklin, John Jay, and John Adams.

The new nation, under the Articles of Confederation and Perpetual Union, was a group of separate states, each with its own government and concentrating on its own interests. The spirit of united action that had joined the colonies during the Revolution had disappeared.

The young states were struggling in confusion. Debts, inflation, and bankruptcy began to mount. With no Army, no Navy, worthless currency, and no government leadership, disintegration started to set in. Faith, trust, and confidence were replaced with a wariness and distrust of one State for another. The reputation of the United States was questionable, its future doubtful. Something would have to be done and done quickly if the United States were to survive.

In May, 1787, a convention of delegates from the various States met in Philadelphia for the purpose of writing a new constitution that would be effective and adequate. In the four months of that convention there was much heated discussion and debate. The delegates were divided in their opinions as to how much authority should be vested in the national government. Some delegates, with Alexander Hamilton as one of the leading protagonists, advocated a strong central government, bordering on a monarchy similar to England, wherein a President would be elected by a few property-holders, and the Governors of the States would be appointed by the President. There were others, including James Madison, who just as firmly believed in the principles expressed by Thomas Jefferson that a strong State government would be best.

A compromise was finally effected. Proportional representation, according to population, would determine the number of members from each State in one legislative branch of the Congress, elected for two years to the House of Representatives. Two members from each State, regardless of size or population, would be elected for six years to the other legislative branch of the Congress, the Senate. Thus, the smaller State need have no fear of any engulfing power of a larger State. Articles 1, 2, and 3 of the new Constitution insured separation of powers of the Executive, Legislative, and Judicial branches of the government. Article 4 provided for the status of the States in the new government and promised to "guarantee to every State in the Union a republican form of government."

Despite these compromises during the framing of the Constitution, difficulties were encountered in its ratification. North Carolina refused to ratify the Constitution without amendments concerning the fundamental rights of human beings. Massachusetts and New Hampshire ratified the Constitution with recommendations for amendments. New York ratified the Constitution reserving the right to secede if her suggested Bill of Rights was not included as an amendment within six years. Because of these many misgivings by the States that national authority might endanger their hard-fought-for individual liberties, the first Congress drew up twelve amendments to the Constitution. Ten of them were ratified by the States.

George Washington became the first President of the United States and was inaugurated on April 30, 1789. He appointed, among others, Thomas Jefferson, Secretary of State, and Alexander Hamilton, Secretary of the Treasury. The immediate concern of the administration was to unravel the complexity of domestic affairs and international relations. Credit had to be established and public debts had to be paid if the country was to become a respected nation at home and abroad. Confidence and faith in its security were the first consideration. Such questions as the admission of new States; the establishment of the Army and the Navy; the development of suit-

able harbors for commerce and defense, of a pos-
tal service and of post roads; the institution of a
new judiciary system; the program of taxation,
of currency, of pensions, of internal and foreign
commerce; many details had to be dealt with so
that the government could function effectively.

Hamilton's policy of funding the national debt
and assuming the debts of the States,* his determination to pay all creditors to the full, the
establishment of a national bank, the levying of
an excise tax and tariff were of significant support to the American manufacturers.

It is interesting to note that, in general, support for the Constitution came from the capital-
ist or manufacturing centers, and the opposition
came from the agrarian groups and those bur-
dened with private debts.†

Within Washington's cabinet, Jefferson and
Hamilton differed in their opinions concerning the
people's participation in governmental affairs.
Jefferson had full confidence and sympathy for
the people as an integral factor in a true democracy. Hamilton, on the other hand, had no confidence in the ability of the masses to govern

---

*President Washington considered the satisfaction of the
public debt the principal reason for the adoption of the Constitution.

†Occupying an influential position in the former of these
classes [capitalist] were the holders of the State and Continental
debts..."[1]

themselves and believed that only the aristocracy was capable of representing the government.

It was Thomas Jefferson who had written the first draft of the Declaration of Independence in which it was stated "that all men are created equal." His long and intensive study of the philosophies of Voltaire, Rousseau, Locke and Montesquieu, among others, determined his program for the establishment of a true democracy. He was convinced that the United States belonged to her people, and these people should actively participate in the conduct of the government. He pressed for laws to ease the restrictions against voting privileges and the removal of class differences. As an owner of large plantations in Virginia, he was aware of the problems of the agrarian interests, and he disapproved of the concentration of large land holdings among the few. Among his leading supporters were James Monroe and James Madison.

Alexander Hamilton had been closely associated with George Washington during the Revolution, having served as his secretary and aide. Washington had developed an admiration and respect for Hamilton, as well as confidence in his judgment during this close association. When Hamilton married the daughter of the wealthy and influential Philip Schuyler of upper New York State, Hamilton's social status advanced to a position comparable with his political sympathies for the wealthy business and property interests. His family connection with the Schuylers also served to his political advantage in New York State politics. John Adams was one of his staunch supporters.

Hamilton and Jefferson were united only in their admiration for Washington. However, disagreements soon arose over the interpretation of the Constitution. Hamilton's loose interpretation displeased Jefferson. The followers of Hamilton began to call themselves Federalists to indicate their belief in a stronger confederation of states. Those who differed with them were referred to as Anti-Federalists. Local political societies were organized, and those who supported Jefferson as their leader named themselves Republicans, or Democrats, or Democrat-Republicans.

In New York State, Jefferson received strong support from Governor George Clinton who was a political enemy of Schuyler, Hamilton's father-in-law. Clinton had been defeated by John Adams in his bid for the Vice-Presidency in the election of 1792 because of Hamilton's influence.

Burr, in New York City, joined with Governor Clinton in opposition to Hamilton. Burr, who had been associated for a short time with Washington and Hamilton during the Revolution, disliked them both and had little respect for either of them as leaders. As the guiding spirit of the Sons of St. Tammany, Burr became a political boss of a clever political machine. As a brilliant lawyer and a shrewd politician with a large following in New York City, Burr exercised a strong influence on city, state, and national politics during this period. By means of the purchase of a small property which listed as its owners all the members of the Sons of St. Tammany, the limitations of the voting franchise were circumvented and he was thus able to control a large number of votes.

During Washington's second administration, England and France went to war. Washington proclaimed the neutrality of this country, but in fact this country was not neutral. England resented that the United States favored the use of her ports by the French and that the United States profited as a result of the British conflict with France. In order to avoid a war, John Jay was sent to England where he effected a treaty that placated the British. The French, however, were highly displeased with Jay's treaty and felt that they had been poorly treated by the country that they had helped. Envoys, sent by the United States to France to negotiate, were received with coldness. Again, the United States was on the brink of war, this time with France.

The early years of the 1790's, with Washington as the first President, were alive with jealousies and bickering among the leaders of the country over matters of national policy. The animosity resulting from personal, factional, and sectional differences resulted in the rise of the political parties and, coincidentally, the political newspaper.

It was the need of the political leaders to spread their favored doctrines widely and forcefully that required them to found their own newspapers. It was primarily to be a device through which issues and differences of political opinion and political personalities could be aired freely according to the sentiments of the founder. The newspapers were controlled by the political leaders and were chiefly political tracts aimed at persuading the people to take sides on political questions.

The issues of the national bank, of the funding of the national debt, of the affects of taxation; whether to join in alliance with England or with France; whether to agree with Hamilton or side with Jefferson on the principles of a strong state government or a strong central government; these were some of the pressing issues dividing the political thought and which the political leaders through their own newspapers were determined to resolve according to their own convictions.

Hamilton was supported by *The Gazette of the United States* edited by John Fenno. Jefferson's political organ was *The National Gazette*, edited by Phillip Freneau. Both Freneau and Fenno had government jobs that were provided for them by their sponsors. Hamilton also gave financial assistance to other editors, including Noah Webster and his *American Minerva* in New York, and to William Cobbett, the "Peter Porcupine" of the *Porcupine Gazette* in Philadelphia. *The Aurora*, under Benjamin Franklin Bache, was another leading Republican organ used as a sounding board by Jefferson and Burr as a method of attacking Federalists. *Greenleaf's New York Journal and Patriotic Register* and the *Argus*, both owned by Thomas Greenleaf, were violently partisan in their attacks on the administration and were Burr's favored instruments of public expression in New York City.

Under such by-lines as "Camillus," "Aristedes," "Brutus," "Cato," "Pacificus" and "Juno," political leaders wrote messages to the newspapers. Often these writings were clipped from one newspaper and reprinted in another. Under this protective anonymity the writers performed unafraid, unrestrained, with intense hostility and with wild denunciations, revealing the depth of the heated emotional involvement in the political arena of that day.

[Hamilton wrote that he was] unequivocally convinced that Mr. Madison, cooperating with Mr. Jefferson, is at the head of a faction, decidedly hostile to me and my administration, and actuated by views of judgement subversive to the principle of good government and dangerous to the Union, peace and happiness of the Country.[2]

Jefferson promptly answered:

.... Mr. Hamilton, that Federalist tax gatherer, that Singular character who was not only a monarchist, but for a monarchy bottomed on corruption, who was so bewitched and perverted by the British example as to be under thorough conviction that corruption was essential to the government of a nation.[3]

Thus did the hireling editors of the political presses perform at the bidding of their leaders. Thus did the different presses create and persuade public opinion during the first decade of the new government, increasing their venom, vituperation, and indiscretion in their statements of news and views and resorting to wild name-calling and distortions of the facts.

In 1798, during John Adams' administration, the government, in an attempt to stem the tide of public opinion wrought by the Republican newspapers and to destroy the effectiveness of their journalistic weapons, passed the Alien and Sedition Laws. A section of these Laws stated:

". . . If any person shall write, print, utter, or publish, or procure to be written, printed, uttered, or published, or shall knowingly or willingly assist or aid in writing, printing, uttering, or publishing any false, scandalous, and malicious writing or writings against the government of the United States, or either house of Congress, or the President of the United States, with intent to defame the said government, or either house of the said Congress, or the said President, or to bring them, or either of them, the hatred of the good people of the United

States, or to stir up therein, for opposing or resisting any law of the United States, or any act of the President of the United States done in pursuance of any law or of the powers in him vested by the Constitution of the United States, or to resist, oppose, or defeat any such law or act, or to aid, encourage, or abet any hostile design of any foreign nation against the United States, their people, or government, then such person, being thereof convicted before any court of the UnitedStates having jurisdiction thereof, shall be punished by a fine not exceeding $2000, and by imprisonment not exceeding two years. . . ."

Several editors were punished under this law, and their pens were stopped. However these laws, imperiling freedom of speech and freedom of the press, provided the ammunition needed by enemies of the Federalist party for a campaign issue in the forthcoming Presidential election of 1800. The election resulted in a tie vote for President between Thomas Jefferson and Aaron Burr, neither of whom was a Federalist.

COLONIAL LONG ISLAND

THE POLITICAL CLIMATE on Long Island following the Revolution was similar to that of the nation. As the other colonists had suffered during the Revolution, so had the Long Islanders, but with one difference. Long Island had been continuously occupied from 1776 to 1783 by the British who regarded Long Island as a strategically situated prize which separated the northern and southern colonies and guarded the waters surrounding the port of New York. When the Revolution ended, the Long Islanders began to repair the devastation wrought by the British occupation and to start a new life.

The history of Long Island, from the early days of its settlement, had been one of change and adjustment. Having left Europe because they desired various freedoms, the Long Islanders found instead the hardships of establishing themselves in a strange and primitive land previously occupied only by Indians, and under the domination of a series of governing bodies which, more or less concerned with personal gain, set restrictions on their freedoms.

The Dutch claimed Long Island on the basis of Henry Hudson's discovery in 1609, under the auspices of the Dutch East India Company. The English claimed ownership to Long Island by right of the discoveries of Sebastian Cabot in 1508-1509.

In 1614 the first Dutch settlers (under the leadership of Adrian Block) arrived on Manhattan Island to establish a trading post with the Indians. On his ship, the *Restless*, Block sailed around Long Island and drew a map of its contours. In 1639, Dutch settlements were established on Manhattan Island, and it was given the name of New Amsterdam. The desire for larger stretches of farm land prompted some of the wealthy Dutch merchants to obtain permission from the West India Company to move across the East River from New Amsterdam and form a new colony at the western end of Long Island. The colony was named Bruijkleen.

Most of the English who came to Long Island were Puritans, having migrated from Massachusetts and Connecticut by way of Long Island Sound and settled on the eastern end of the Island. In 1640, the towns at the east end of Long Island became a part of Connecticut and with her joined the union of the Puritan colonies of New England in 1643. At that time, a Constitution was drawn up, the Preamble of which read in part: "We all came to these parts of America with one and the same aim, namely, to advance the Kingdom of our Lord Jesus Christ, and to enjoy the liberties of the gospel in purity and peace."

Though the English and the Dutch were aware of each other's settlements on Long Island, they did not interfere with each other. The Dutch continued to settle at the west end, and the English continued to settle at the east end of the Island, and, at first, there was ample room for both. However, as time went on, and the settlements grew and spread, it became necessary to set a boundary. In 1650, at a meeting in Hartford, Connecticut, the official division between the Dutch and the English colonies was drawn at the westernmost part of Oyster Bay, south in a direct line to the sea, all land to the west of the line to be Dutch, all land to the east to be English.

In 1664, when the English captured New Amsterdam, all of Long Island became an English colony under the control of the Duke of York and Albany. The Royal Letters Patent under which James, Duke of York and Albany, acquired title to Long Island empowered the Duke to establish a government in which he was endowed with almost complete sovereign control. Under the same Royal Letters Patent, Charles II cut off the eastern end of Long Island from Connecticut politically, and joined it to New York. Thus, in August 1664, the people of Long Island were subjected to a rigid and oppressive government under the Duke of York and Albany. Those at the eastern end who had previously enjoyed comparative independence particularly resented the change of rule in government. The change was not to their liking and they objected vigorously.

In 1665 there was a meeting in Hempstead of delegates from all the towns on Long Island at which time the Duke's Laws were approved. The people had been betrayed by their delegates. The promise that had been made to them by the British when they defeated the Dutch in New York that they would enjoy the same privileges as the other Royal colonies in North America had been violated.

In answer to these protests, Governor Nicholls threatened to punish severely any individual who criticized those who signed the Address to his Royal Highness.

The first stirring of resentment against English rule had begun on Long Island.

Francis Lovelace, who succeeded Governor Nicholls, was primarily concerned with raising revenue and imposed heavy taxes upon the young colony. And so, at the very beginning of English rule in New York, the cry of "Taxation without representation" was heard.

Under the rule of Colonel Andros, similar exploitation continued combined with extravagance and cruelty. Other Colonial Governors pursued the same course, levying taxes at their own dictation and ignoring the cries of protest to which the people reacted as each new injustice was initiated.

The clamor of the people for representation continued, and in 1682 they finally received some satisfaction. The Duke of York consulted William Penn who convinced him to submit to the will of the people so that they may be free. The concession on the part of the Duke of York to permit a Representative Assembly was by no means a voluntary one granted in the spirit of benevolence. The concession was granted when the Duke sensed that the people had reached the breaking point in their resistance against his tyranny.

The first Colonial legislature was composed of a Governor and his Council and seventeen members selected by the people. Courts were established and some changes were made in the Duke's Laws. Long Island was split up into three counties of Kings, Queens and Suffolk.

When the Duke of York became King of Enland in 1685, as James II, he dissolved the Assemblies, forbade the use of a printing press, and sent soldiers to Long Island to suppress any expression of opposition that might arise. He forbade trade with Europe and India, all merchandise first having to be directed through England for payment of import and export duties. All other commerce had to be directed through the Port in New York. Consequently, the embittered and defiant east-enders, who found it too costly to have to deliver their merchandise about one hundred miles back to New York, engaged in smuggling. They continued their trade with Massachusetts, Connecticut, and Rhode Island, with whom they still felt a close kinship, by slipping in and out of the many coves along the north shore.

Whaling played an important role in the development of Long Island and began with its early settlers. It became a flourishing industry at the east end of the Island. The colonists were further harassed in 1696, when along with the other taxes and inconveniences, whales were declared "royal fish," and like everything else in the colonies were the property of the mother country. Samuel Mulford, an East Hampton whaler, went to London and addressed the House of Commons. He appealed for a Port to be established at Sag Harbor, and he was largely responsible for Sag Harbor becoming such a Port of Entry, paying taxes to the Crown.

With the advantage of the Port at Sag Harbor, commerce boomed at the east end of Long Island, and the settlements began to prosper. A list of the exports in 1747 included beer, pork, tallow, Indian corn, staves, shingles, hoops, anchor stocks, onions, horses, and sheep. Imports included molasses, rum, cocoa, and Spanish gold coins. The whale oil that had been so eagerly sought by the British was still being shipped in much greater quantity to Boston than to New York.

When War broke out in Lexington, Massachusetts, in 1775, Long Island was divided in its sympathies. Kings County, whose people were Dutch, was indifferent to the plight of the Massachusetts colony and preferred to remain neutral in that battle. A war would mean sacrifice, loss of money, and possibly their homes. Queens County was mixed in its sentiments. There were ardent Royalists who were loyal to the King, and ardent Patriots who were eager for separation from England. There was also a large Quaker population in Queens who were for peace at any price. Suffolk County was almost unanimous in its desire for independence, bitter in its feelings against England, and ready and anxious to fight and fight hard for the cause of freedom.

The Patriots drew up the Articles of Association for the common defense, and organized weekly meetings for military training. This was signed in August, 1775.

The Articles of Association read, in part:

Shocked by the Bloody scene now enacting in Massachusetts Bay, . . . [we who are] resolved never to become slaves, Do associate under all the ties of Religion, Honor, and Love to our country to adopt and Endeavor to carry into Execution whatever measure may be recommended by the Continental Congress or resolved upon by our Provincial Convention of preserving our Constitution and oppose the Execution of the several arbitrary and Oppressive Acts of the British Parliament until a reconciliation between Great Britain and America on Constitutional Principles 'which we most violently desire can be obtained' and that we will in all things follow the advice of our General Committee respecting the good order and the safety of individuals and private property.

General Washington had anticipated that after their evacuation from Boston, the British would move next to New York, and so Kings County was ordered to cooperate with Colonel Ward in the fortification of Brooklyn Heights. A committee was ordered to use force on any man who refused to help in the defense of Brooklyn.

On July 5, 1776, the day after the signing of the Declaration of Independence in Philadelphia, General Howe established British headquarters on Staten Island. General Green, who was originally in command of the American forces in Brooklyn and who knew the area thoroughly, became ill. He was replaced by General Putnam who, on such short notice could not acquaint himself with the problems of his command. Because of the defection of some Loyalists, the British had a thorough knowledge of the terrain, its highways and byways. The colonists were overwhelmed and Washington and his troops were forced to a hasty retreat by ferry to Manhattan Island.

On August 27, 1776, the British took possession and established their headquarters in Brooklyn. The army spread out over neighboring towns and several other towns to the east on the Island. Long Island was an important vantage point of occupation for the British inasmuch as it guarded the approach to New York from its many surrounding waters. It was a military prize of great value and one to be held under its control at all costs as Long Island separated the northern and the southern colonies from communication by sea. The British remained there until the Treaty of Paris was signed in 1783.

Southampton, East Hampton, Sag Harbor, and the other east end towns were stranded and unprotected when most of their young men joined Washington's army. Many people in these towns fled to Connecticut, which was still safe and free. And so the exodus from Long Island began. In September, 1776, the port of Sag Harbor became the scene of great activity as refugees embarked to Connecticut and safety. Those who could afford to left at once. Others waited, in the hope of protecting property, but left as danger forced them out. There were those unfortunates who did not have the means to flee after the Battle of Long Island and were left behind to face the wrath of the British occupation as a penalty for signing the Articles of Association in 1775. If they had to remain at home to tend to the aged or the infirm, they were required to swear allegiance to Great Britain.*

The British occupation of Long Island was a terrible time for those who remained at home—a

---

*"The stigma placed upon those who remained at home, because they were too poor to seek safety eleswhere, has subjected the Revolutionary families to the scorn of the people on the mainland, and has placed an undeserved blot on the settlement".[4]

terrible time and a sad time. Families were separated as men left for Connecticut to serve the Patriot cause. During the British occupation, property was wantonly taken, stolen or destroyed. In 1778, Governor Tryon and 1200 soldiers traveled from one end of the Island to the other and took all the cattle, grain and provisions that lay in their path. Some farmers in desperation hid their poultry, sheep and swine in their cellars in an attempt to salvage some sustenance for themselves. Corporal punishment was administered at the slightest provocation. With the British taking possession of whatever they desired, even the homes and services of the colonists were surrendered without protest lest the colonists be punished as disloyal traitors. There was nothing they could call their own as they lived in privation and in fear.

A spy ring formed by Gen. Washington was active on Long Island and did much to assist him as head of the Continental Army. It must be remembered that during the British occupation, with soldiers quartered in their homes and Tory sympathizers everywhere, the Patriots were always under observation. But, as the Patriots were observed, so did they also observe. Communications were sent by letter in code using invisible ink, an invention of John Jay. Among the Patriots, one means of communication was the use of different colors and kinds of clothing supposedly airing or drying on the clothesline.

The entire story of the spy activities on Long Island is not known, but it has been established that Robert Townsend, as Culper, Jr., with the help of his sister, Sarah, at Raynham Hall in Oyster Bay, was responsible for the detection of Benedict Arnold's treason at West Point. Abraham Woodhull, of Setauket, was known to Washington as Culper, Sr. Caleb Brewster traveled back and forth across the Sound in the guise of a fisherman and served as a link with the Connecticut Patriots.

The Long Island Patriots who had escaped to Connecticut did not sit back quietly and wait for the war to end. They became a part of the Connecticut forces and by means of the spy network on Long Island arranged to harass the British troops at frequent intervals. Though they were mostly untrained farmers, they had the advantage of their thorough knowledge of every cove and inlet on the Island so that they were able to attack in the dead of night. Their desire to seek vengeance on the British who had desecrated their land gave them the courage to court danger in daring guerilla tactics.

The battle of Sag Harbor was a daring surprise attack by Lieutenant Colonel Meigs and 234 Long Island refugee whalers who crossed over from New Haven to Southold in 1777 and made their way through woods, marshes, and water in the dark of night and succeeded in dealing a heavy blow to the British. They destroyed brigs, sloops, and vessels that were standing in the harbor, as well as tons of hay, rum, and other provisions. Ninety of the British occupation troops were killed and many more were taken prisoner. All the Americans returned to Connecticut and safety. In 1780, Captain Tallmadge with the aid of fifty men came over from Connecticut to Coram and set fire to several tons of hay which had been stored for winter forage. In 1781, Major Lemuel Prescott, with about one hundred men from the Fifth Connecticut Regiment and the Second Continental Dragoons sailed across the Sound and destroyed Fort Salonga without the loss of a single man.

The estimated loss to Long Islanders as a result of the British occupation was one-half million dollars. In addition they were forced to suffer the indignities of a prolonged and severe occupation. The final blow came after the war was over and the New York State Legislature taxed the Long Islanders $95,000 (Suffolk was taxed $50,000) because "they did not take an active part in the war against the enemy."

Not only were those Long Islanders who stayed at home punished for not taking "an active part in the war against the enemy," but those who fled to Connecticut as well. Many shipping families, including John and Samuel Foster, Daniel and Nathan Fordham, John Hud-

son, etc. took their ships with them when they
fled to Connecticut and became privateers attacking British ships. They contributed the booty
to the Patriots to be sold for clothing and ammunition. The war had taken a large toll on their
fortunes and when they returned home they were
in debt. John Foster, for example, was a dele-
gate to the first Provincial Congress. He was on
the Committee of Safety and an auditor of all
claims of those who fought with Colonel Smith
at the Battle of Long Island. He lost a ship worth
$10,000 that was destroyed by the British, and
upon his return to Sag Harbor from Connecticut
in 1783, after the British had evacuated he was
imprisoned for debt. His plea that his ship, house
barn and outhouses, as well as goods, books and
papers had been destroyed by the enemy during
the occupation was not considered.

After the War, Long Islanders started to return to their homes and face the destruction
left in the wake of the British occupation. The
majority had to rehabilitate their homes and
towns with a minimum of material and money.
Life was to be a struggle for many years after the
War was over. The Long Islanders settled down
as free people to the grim business of earning a
living.

Mills and factories started to operate once
again on the Island. The Brown Brothers Pottery
Works opened in Huntington; the Jones family

opened a wool factory in Cold Spring Harbor; Roslyn boasted a paper mill and a grist mill. Schools were built. Farmers, with the help of Ezra L'Hommedieu of Long Island and Robert Livingston of Hudson Valley, were encouraged to plant new crops.

The whaling industry began anew and the Port of Sag Harbor became busy once again. Sag Harbor is located in the northwest corner of the town of Southampton, one hundred miles from New York City. The village is on the south shore of Shelter Island Sound. Deep channels run close to the shore at Sag Harbor and it is an excellent deep-water port. Its harbor is protected against storm by Shelter Island. Until 1730 there had been no permanent settlers there. At that time Nathan Fordham, James Foster, and James Howell built homes down by the Landing.

There was a fortune to be made in whaling in those days. The whale oil lamp was used universally. The leather tanning trade needed whale oil. A barrel sold for $29.00. Whale bone (from the mouth only) was used for hoop skirts and corset stays. No doubt it was the increasing value of the whale products that prompted the Hampton settlers to build piers at Sag Harbor. As a port it was within communicable distance with New York and New England.

Sag Harbor became a Port of Entry by Act of Congress on August 10, 1790, in the second session of the first Congress of the United States which was held in New York City. As a seaport, measured by its trade and shipping, it was second only to the Port of New York. It was named a Port of Entry in the same bill that established the Port of New York. Sag Harbor residents were proud to note that Sag Harbor was mentioned before New York in that Act. Henry Packer Dering was appointed Collector of the Port by George Washington.

With the first Port on the Island, the first post office, and the flourishing whale industry aiding the growth of the town, it appeared that Sag Harbor was destined to become a thriving metropolis. Henry Dering, Collector of the Port and Postmaster, and others, felt, therefore, the need of a printer and a printing press. He encouraged David Frothingham of Boston to come to Sag Harbor, and on May 10, 1791, the first issue of the first Long Island newspaper, *Frothingham's Long Island Herald*, was published. Dering was aware that "the printing press is a social instrument, especially in the regular production of a newspaper. It keeps the diary of the community, maintains a forum for its discussions, and provides an exchange for its commerce."[5]

As the town grew and prospered in the last decade of the eighteenth century, it appeared that the people had settled down at last to a life of personal freedom and pursuit of happiness. It must be borne in mind that these people who had fought against the British for these rights, and who had suffered severe personal hardships during the Revolution, would be ever watchful and suspicious of any possibility that these rights might be in jeopardy. They were interested and concerned when the new government was formed. They were eager for information on national affairs, domestic and foreign, as well as on the affairs of the government within New York State. With the advantages of a newspaper and of boats that brought them news from other places, they felt they were in a position to guard their newly found liberties.

In a letter from Selleck Osborn to Henry Packer Dering, dated December 9, 1801, in which he expressed an interest in printing the newspaper at Sag Harbor, the following excerpt sums up the sentiments of the people:

It has been frequently intimated that a Republican Printer would meet with a welcome reception in the town where you reside, and with good encouragement throughout the County of Suffolk.[6]

PART II   *Chapter Three*
DAVID FROTHINGHAM

IT WAS IN SUCH AN atmosphere and at such a time that David Frothingham came to Sag Harbor to establish the first printing press on Long Island. In the preface to *David Frothingham, the First Printer of Long Island*, written by his great-great-grandson, Louis Tooker Vail, the following is noted:

To compile a biography of David Frothingham . . . is a weighty task at this date. Records have been lost, and some willfully destroyed, due, it is thought, to political as well as private enmity.[7]

An analysis of known data concerning Frothingham sheds insight into the struggles and conflicts that gripped Colonial America during his lifetime. He might be considered a product of his generation. He might also be considered one of its victims.

The Frothingham family can be traced back in English history to the time of Henry VIII. The first Frothingham to arrive in America was William who came here in 1630 with John Winthrop and his colonizing entourage and settled in Charlestown, Massachusetts. The Frothinghams were a large family, and their men were prominent among the citizens of the town serving in the clergy and participating actively in civic affairs. The Frothingham property was adjacent to that of the Bunker property in the area of Edes Street.

David Frothingham was born in Charlestown Massachusetts, on October 8, 1765. Charlestown is the second oldest town in Massachusetts across the Charles River from Boston. His father, David, who was a mariner and in the military service, died in 1766, one year after young David was born. After David's father died, his mother, Hannah (nee Gibson) married Benjamin C. Bunker on August 11, 1767. It is recorded that Benjamin Bunker's estate was administered in June, 1774. In 1775, Hannah married again, this time to Richard Trumbull.

The Frothingham family motto *Servabo Fidem*, "I Will Preserve The Faith" characterized the family activities in the New World. The town records of Charlestown for this early period frequently mention the Frothinghams and their participation in the colony's conflict with England during the Pre-Revolutionary crises.

The Stamp Act was passed on March 22, 1765, and was intended to be effective as of November 1, 1766. On September 11 of that year a petition of protest that "several acts of Parliament have a direct tendency to distress the trade and commerce of this province, and in our opinion, to deprive us of our rights and privi-

leges granted by royal charter" was signed by
Nathaniel Frothingham.[8] On the tea issue John
Frothingham and others were instructed to "in-
quire whether any of the inhabitants of the town
had imported or bought or sold goods contrary
to the agreement of the merchants of Boston,"[9]
and, furthermore, "to consult with the select-
men of Boston . . . to prevent the use of foreign
tea among us."[10] At a meeting on February 9,
1770, Nathaniel Frothingham and two others
were to obtain "the names of such inhabitants
as had determined to leave off the use of foreign
tea in their families," and also, "such as refused
to comply and lay same before the town at the
adjournment of the meeting."[11]

Deacon Frothingham and Nathaniel Frothingham were on a committee "to wait on the
sellers of tea and desire them to leave off selling
the article, as it would be the means to promote
the public good."[12] Nathaniel Frothingham was
a selectman in 1771 and 1772.

A petition of November 24, 1773, declaring
that "being duly alarmed with the report of a
large quantity of tea soon to be imported into
this Province by the East India Company,"
called a meeting "to discuss these critical and
distressing circumstances."[13] John Frothingham's name was on the top line leading the list
of signatures.

And so, starting with William Frothingham, one of the original settlers, who was one of the founders of the church and was often associated with the town affairs, down through the years of the growing colony, the Frothingham family continued its activities in civic affairs in uninterrupted success from one generation to the next.

This, then was the climate in which David Frothingham lived during his early years, In 1775-1776, during the Battles of Lexington and Concord, Bunker Hill, and the siege of Boston, David was between nine and ten years of age. There can be no doubt of his close contact with active rebellion and political activity, as well as with the hostilities of the War itself. It is probable that a stirring of social consciousness and opinion developed at this time concerning American independence and English rule including an antagonism toward England set by the example of his father's family. This background may have been a determining factor in the choice of a career in which he would be in a position to influence public opinion. He studied to be a printer in Boston.

When he was nineteen years old, he eloped with Nancy Pell, the daughter of Joseph Pell, an extremely wealthy landowner of Pelham Manor, New York. Nancy was sixteen at the time of their marriage and was promptly disowned by her irate father who did not approve of the marriage of his daugther to a penniless printer.

They had been married seven years at the time of his arrival in Sag Harbor some time between February 7, 1791 and May 10, 1791, to establish a printing office, a book store, and a bindery near the Landing at the foot of Main Street. The building used by Frothingham for his business was built in 1735 by John Foster, one of the earliest settlers of the town.

On Tuesday, May 10, 1791, the first issue of *Frothingham's Long Island Herald* was printed by David Frothingham at Sag Harbor. It was the first newspaper printed on Long Island and was the only newspaper on Long Island for eight years. In June, 1799, Thomas Kirk, a bookseller and printer, issued *The Courier and New York and Long Island Advertiser* in Brooklyn. Sag Harbor was the eighth point in New York State outside of New York City in which a press was set in operation.

PART II *Chapter Four*

LONG ISLAND HERALD

THE ONLY INFORMATION on the story of how Frothingham came to Sag Harbor is obtained from two original letters in the files of the Penny-packer Collection at the Easthampton Library, in Easthampton, Long Island.

The first letter, dated January 25, 1791, and addressed to Henry P. Dering* reads as follows:

Sir
Agreeable to my promise I have enquired of Mr. Payne respecting Mr. Frothingham's Proposals—but he could give me no information—I also called at Mr. Frothingham's Lodgings the day Capt. Satterly left this place, but he was not then in town— I saw him today & received the enclosed proposals.—He informs me that he expects to set out for S. Harbor about 3 Weeks hence, and will fix his residence wherever the majority of his subscribers think proper—

from Sir your friend and Hum'Serv
David Gardiner Jr.[16]

---

*Henry P. Dering, the first Collector of the Port for the United States at Sag Harbor was probably one of the leading citizens of the town. "He was both intelligent and active, and was esteemed by all as a person of the strictest integrity" [14] Besides being the Collector of the Port, he later became the first Postmaster on Long Island, and was part owner of a thriving business as well. That he was a staunch Republican can be determined from a letter sent to him by Selleck Osborn, in 1801, when he negotiated for the transfer of the newspaper to him.[15] His grandfather, Henry Dering, had been the first to introduce the manufacture of paper in New England, and therein may be a clue to the source of paper used by Frothingham's press.

The second letter, written by David Frothnigham to Henry Dering, indicates that there had been many discussions with various emissaries and that Frothingham had confidence in the future of the village of Sag Harbor and his own prospects as a printer there:

New York, Feb. 7, 1791

Dear Sir:

I called on Mr. Gelston, your Assemblyman, the other evening and he informed me, that you were making great exertions for me, for which, sir, I give you my most hearty thanks. He said that I had as near as he could guess, about 350 subscribers, provided I would settle in Sagg Harbour. I would now inform you that I should have no objections, provided the respectable inhabitants of Sagg Harbour would give the greatest encouragement. I received a Letter from the Rev. Mr. Buell which mentioned that, The Trustees of the Academy would provide me a place to live in, &c. and that I could find none in your town——a stationers shop he said would meet with encouragement — and that nothing on his part, and Dr. Sage's should be wanting to encourage the press in every point of view. I have never seen the place, therefore can form no idea but as I am told that Sagg Harbour is the place of trade, we may suppose, that like the *Centre of Gravity* it draws most of the inhabitants around to it.—Therefore East Hampton would be out of the way—Capt. Latham told me that he doubted not, but I would meet with encouragement, but Sagg Harbour must be my station. It is a custom as ancient as the *noble art of printting* that when a young beginner sets up his business in a Country place to have some small premium, such as wood &c. as the great expense often strips him of all his Cash, unless he has as the old proverb, verified 'Born with a silver spoon in his mouth.'

I take the Liberty of writing this freely, as the character I have had of you, sir, attaches me very

much to you; and I flatter myself that you will not
take umbrage at it—It is a duty we owe all mankind to
'*Lend a helping hand.*' You doubtless are apprised of
the advantage a press would be in your town, and as a
friend to literature I doubt not but you will do everything in your power to forward the undertaking. Please
to write me as expeditious as possible, how many subscribers I have really got and as you are acquainted
with the minds of the people, can give me a satisfactory
return. After the first quarter shall have no objection
to receive any kind of produce in payment, and try to
make everything agreeable to my generous patrons—
I remain, Dear sir, your unknown friend and well-
wisher

DAVID FROTHINGHAM

N.B. I shall wait with impatience until I get an answer,
pray write by the first vessel or opportunity——[17]

This letter reveals the degree of understanding required between a printer and his sponsor,
the need for financial help on the part of the printer, and the promise "to make everything agreeable to my generous patrons in return.

In the first issue of the *Herald*, dated May 10,
1791, David Frothingham wrote a letter in which
he stated his aims, ideals, and format for his paper which was to be published once a week:

TO THE PUBLIC

With the greatest deference the first Number of the
HERALD is laid before the Public, on whose smiles
the Editor founds his hope of patronage, and expects
so laudable an undertaking will meet with encouragement tantamount to its merits. Too much puffing frequently is made use of by publishers, but when the Editor shall cease to merit applause, he will no longer wish
the favor of the public attended to him. Neither diligence nor labor shall be wanting to render this paper

a useful repository of knowledge, humour and entertainment, while Vice, the bane of society, with its concomitant attendants, though clothed with the garb of
authority, will be branded with every mark of infamy.
Whatever had a tendency to expand the mind and embelish the understanding will be prosecuted with in-
defatigable zeal; and every branch of literature ransacked to enlighten and enlarge the human mind; in a
word, we shall

'Eye Nature's walks, shoot folly as it flies,
And catch the manners living as they rise.'

In the course of this publication a corner will be devoted to the treasures of those in the Poetic line, whose
correspondence together with those in the prosaic walk
are earnestly requested.

DAVID FROTHINGHAM[18]

Thus, with becoming humility and modesty
did the first Long Island printer state his standards for good journalism, promise to fulfill and
maintain these standards, and establish an understanding with his readers for success in his
new venture. A quotation from Alexander Pope's
Essay on Man, "Eye Nature's Walks, Shoot Folly
as it Flies,— And Catch the Manners living as
They Rise," was printed under the masthead as
the motto.

In accordance with his stated aims, the first
issue contained items of philosophy; morals;
poetry on Religion, on Humanity, and on Gratitude to God for Providential Mercies; anecdotes;
reprints from *The Farmer's, Christian's,* and
Scholar's Magazine of agricultural news; and advice on how to prevent UNHAPPY MAR-
RIAGES. The news items were reprints from old

newspapers.   The foreign news was dated January 10, from London. American affairs contained news from Charlestown, South Carolina, dated April 3; from Philadelphia, dated April 20; from Worcester, dated April 21; and from New Haven, dated April 27.

The issue of May 10, 1791, contained nine* advertisements advising its readers of the following: 1) Phineas DuVall had lost a dog with a white breast and white feet, and the finder would be offered a handsome reward. 2) Ephraim L.' Hommedieu ran a packet to New London every week. 3) Silas Raymond had a tailoring establishment. 4) Asa Partridge had a 'Young Lady's School' and "these gentlemen who please to send their children to be educated here, may depend on having their morals and manners carefully inspected by their very humble servant."[19]

The newspaper consisted of four pages of rather small print. With the exception of the advertisements, it contained no mention of local Sag Harbor news. The first issue of the Frothingham press has been considered as "a model of typographical excellence and neatness."[20]

Frothingham in his endeavors to increase his circulation, announced on June 14, 1791 that a

---

*The five advertisements not enumerated were notices from the Printing Office, and are discussed in greater detail in Part III.

post rider with headquarters at New York City at Benjamin Strong and Company, 37 Water Street, had been employed to travel through the Island.[21] This was customary practice with most country printers. "Subscribers usually received their papers from the post rider, who made a weekly journey through the country, dispensing newspapers, carrying mail in the absence of a regular mail service, and performing sundry errands for the people on his route."[22] A further bid for increased circulation of his newspaper was indicated by the following announcement on June 21, 1791:

TO THE PUBLIC

The subscriber, having established a Printing Office at Sagg-Harbour and employed a Post to ride through the Island to New York, earnestly requests the assistance, and patronage of the Inhabitants of Long Island, and New York, to enable him in the support of his infant establishment.

Subscriptions will be taken at every place where the papers are left, and at every public house on the road to New York. In New York, by Jacob Conkling, near Fly-Market, and by Benjamin Strong & Co. No. 37 Water Street, Where all letters, packages, and commands may be left, as the Post will call to leave and take whatever may be offered to his Charge. Having a careful and attentive man as post-rider, he cannot but hope that there will be no complaint of neglect in the conveyance of letters &c. delivered to his Charge.

As the trade of this part of the Island is now considerable, and is daily increasing, gentlemen in the mercantile line in New York, will find their interest in advertising in this paper. All orders in that way will be punctually attended to by the Publics humble Servant.

DAVID FROTHINGHAM[23]

That this bid for business brought some measure of success can be gleaned from the fact that New York advertising began to appear in the newspaper. On August 9, 1791, for instance, there was an advertisement of an Ironmongery and Cutlery at No. 43 Corner Queen Street and Beekman Slip, New York, and another for Benjamin Strong at 17 Water Street, New York, who sold spices and wine. Furthermore, "on account of the convenience of sending our papers by the Stage, we have altered our publication date to Monday."[24]

The problem of an adequate paper supply was one that Frothingham permitted his readers to share with him. His source of paper is not known. The first papermaking in New York State was in Hempstead in 1768. The Roslyn paper mill was established in 1773. As has been stated, Henry Dering's grandfather was the first to introduce a paper mill in New England. From whatever source the paper was obtained, a sufficient supply of it apparently was a problem, and it was a problem that Frothingham shared with most country printers.

"Since the printer usually chose his location because of the population and political advantages in the area to be served, rather than because of proximity to a paper mill, he encountered numerous difficulties in procuring his supply of paper."[25]

Besides the lack of proximity to the source of paper, money and material for the paper was another problem to face.   Almost every issue of the *Herald* contained one or more advertisements asking for rags, old nets and sailcloths.

On August 23, 1791, there was a two-column article containing an appeal for rags, which read in part:

... Though of small use to the families who may collect them, will still amount to something; and if no more than sufficient to purchase a Bible or Testament will however be better than to sweep out of the doors, or into the fire. Flour may well be produced without wheat, as paper without rags. It therefore behooves every friend to his country, to contribute his endeavors to promote the paper manufactory. It not only retains money in the country, but employs great numbers of its inhabitants.[26]

Frothingham continued his policy of advising his readers of this constant problem, in the hope of enlisting their cooperation in supplying him with the necessary rags:

This week completes twelve months since the commencement of this paper, but as the Printer was deficient (owing to being out of paper) it will be two weeks before the first volume of the 'Herald' will be completed. With a grateful heart he returns thanks for his customers for the encouragement of the year past, and assures them that nothing will be wanting on his part to render a useful and entertaining repository.[27]

The problem of an adequate paper supply continued to plague Frothingham through the years of the *Herald's* history. An advertisement in June 1797 for "A COPY of a LETTER written by OUR SAVIOUR" listed the price per copy at "3 lbs of Rags or a sixpence."[28] In the same year, the following item was written by Frothingham to his public in explanation:

Printer would inform the Patrons of the Herald that although the paper on which it is printed is of smaller size than common yet it contains equal if not more useful matter than many papers printed on a larger size. Larger paper is expected every moment.[29]

From the above notice, it can be concluded that Frothingham did not manufacture the paper himself and that it was delivered to him.

An advertisement was inserted in the issue of November 1, 1791, "Wanted, An Apprentice at the Printing Office."[30] It was answered by John M. Elliott, a local boy whose father was a watchmaker at Sag Harbor. Elliott remained with Frothingham and his press for the entire time that Frothingham lived in Sag Harbor. There is some question as to whether Elliott continued to print the paper after Frothingham's departure from Sag Harbor. On the one hand, there are no copies extant of the *Herald* after December 17, 1798. On the other hand, Milton Hamilton, who made a very detailed study of the country printers of New York State of this early period, noted that after 1798, Elliott printed the *Herald* "in absence of David Frothingham— name not on imprint."[31] Morton Pennypacker, whose collection of Frothingham material at the Easthampton Free Library indicates intensive research and study, believed that the newspaper stopped publication with the issue of December 17, 1798.[32] Yet a letter written by Selleck Osborn to Henry Dering during his negotiations for the purchase of the newspaper mentioned that Osborn expected "young Elliott"[33] to continue his role in the printing office. Since the evidence is conflicting on this point, the conclusion must be left in abeyance.

In the issue of July 9, 1798, the cost of a subscription to the *Herald* was mentioned.

The Conditions of the Herald are, Ten Shillings per Annum, one half at the time of subscribing, the other at the Year's end. Gentlemen wishing to take this impartial vehicle of intelligence by paying ONE DOLLAR in advance, shall be supplied ONE YEAR.[34]

Besides cash, Frothingham let it be known that "any kind of country produce will be taken for this Paper, at the market price."[35] Additional revenue aside from the return from the sale of the newspaper was derived from advertisements, job printing, Log Books for the shipping interests,* local notices paid for by individuals, as well as County and legal advertising which the law required to be printed in the nearest newspaper.

Frothingham's press published many books which were advertised in the *Herald*, and Frothingham is credited with having published the

*The Log Book of Jonathan Osborne is among the Frothingham material at the Morton Pennypacker Long Island Collection in the Easthampton Free Library, Easthampton, New York.

first book on Long Island.* He also advertised re-
gularly that he did book-binding. In this he again
enlisted the cooperation of his readers in his frequent calls for sheepskins and hogskins.

Frothingham launched another, but short-
lived, venture in June, 1796, he published the
"*Long Island Magazine, or Universal Repository*,"
the first magazine published on Long Island.
Only one issue of this magazine was printed, and
it contained fifty-six pages. It included An Address to the Public, twenty-eight articles on various subjects, ten political essays, and foreign and
domestic news. This magazine was probably a
group of selections from the *Herald* and was printed in the same printing office as the newspaper.
The last known copy of this magazine has been
either lost or mislaid in the Jermain Memorial
Library in Sag Harbor.

Despite its many activities, Frothingham's
press apparently ran into financial difficulties.

---

*There seems to be a difference of opinion as to which was
the first book published by Frothingham's press. Overton cre-
dits *An Oration on the Rights of Animals*, by Herman Daggett,
Candidate for the Master's Degree.[36] Pelletreau give this dis-
tinction to *A Plain and Serious Address to the Master of a Family
on the Important Subject of Family Religion*, by Phillip Dodd-
ridge, D. D.[37] A third opinion is offered by William Wallace
Tooker who claims that the first book published by Frothingham was *Verses Occasioned by the Loss of the Brig Sally on Ea-
ton's Neck. together with the reflections said to be made by Capt.
Keeler during the Storm*.[38] These books were all published by
David Frothingham during the year 1791.

Early in 1797 David Frothingham mortgaged his "old press" for thirty pounds sterling to Henry Dering, John Fordham, and Jessie Hodges. Furthermore, in the issue of July 23, 1798, it is noted that "the prospects of the Editor have brightened very much within a few weeks to his subscription list."[39] In August of that year, the following advertisement was inserted in the *Herald*:

> Wanted: A number of small sums of Money from
> 5s to 15s. Inquire of the Printer.[40]

Whether "prospects of the Editor have brightened" and how much is not known, nor the reason for the advertisement wanting "small sums of money." What is known, however, is that David Frothingham printed the last known copy of *Frothingham's Long Island Herald* on Monday, December 17, 1798. It was marked Vol. 7, No. 317.

On Wednesday, December 19, 1798, he attended the Political Rally at Bridgehampton and never returned to Sag Harbor.

TRIAL AND CONVICTION

DECEMBER 19, 1798, was a memorable day for Long Island, and it was a memorable day for David Frothingham as well. It was the day of the Political Rally at Bridgehampton, and the start of the Presidential campaign for Thomas Jefferson on Long Island. David Frothingham attended the Rally and while he was there he met Aaron Burr.

Greenleaf's New York Journal and Patriotic Register presented the following account of the Rally:

Bridgehampton's Big Day, Dec. 22, 1798.

On Wednesday, the 19th instant, . . . was planted a Liberty Tree amidst the acclamations of a large concourse of people who had assembled on the occasion, it is seventy six feet high bearing on top a vane with Liberty inscribed on one side, upon the other side a Spread Eagle with the flag of the United States and a Liberty Cap. It bears, likewise, the following motto, displaying the sentiments of the people, viz.

Vox Populi, vox dei

Amendments, but no infringements upon the Constitution, No unconstitutional act, no unequal taxes, Liberty of the Press, speech, and sentiment, December 19, '98. After it was erected, was sung the celebrated song of the "Liberty Tree" with some small alterations to make it more suitable to the present times, after which the following patriotic toasts were drank.,

TOASTS

1.The Tree of Liberty; may it be watered by the dreams of true Republicanism, take root and flourish, till Kings are not known and tyranny with despotism shall be obliterated . (3 cheers)

2. The People of the United States, may the Genius of Liberty protect their Independence and may they never resign its blessings but with death. (3 cheers)

3. The Constitution of our Country, may we never suffer it to be violated, but may the wisdom of the people, soon see the necessity of further amendments.

4. Thomas Jefferson, our worthy Vice-President; may his republican Virtues, bless our Country, by raising him soon to the first office of government and may the tongue and hand of the slanderer who would injure his honest fame be palsied. (6 cheers)

Toasts were drunk to George Washington, to the men who lost their lives in the War for Independence, to George Clinton and Jonathan N. Havens, to Edward Livingston, and to other Republican Representatives in the Congress of the United States.

Among those present at the Bridgehampton Rally that momentous day were the notable opponents of the Federalists, including Aaron Burr who was combining his political and legal activities while he was there. He had come out to the neighboring town of Easthampton in the role of attorney to Ebenezer Dayton, and had accompanied him to the Rally. Aaron Burr recognized David Frothingham at the Rally and engaged him in conversation. Frothingham was urged to leave Sag Harbor and come to New York to assist Aaron Burr in publishing the *Argus*.

The *Argus* was a newspaper which was owned by Mrs. Thomas Greenleaf whose husband had died during the yellow fever epidemic of 1798.

Perhaps it was the need for money that motivated Frothingham to leave Sag Harbor. Perhaps it was ambition for greater glory in a profession that was enjoying a heyday of reckless power. Perhaps it was the persuasive tongue of Aaron Burr and the excitement of being recognized by such a renowned public figure. Or, perhaps it was the opportunity that he felt would place him in an advantageous position to promote the ideals in which he believed. Whatever the motive may have been that prompted his immediate removal to New York City on that date, Frothingham went to work in New York City and left his family in Sag Harbor. He became the foreman of the *Argus* at eight dollars per week.

Both the *Argus* and *Greenleaf's New York Journal and Patriotic Register* were published by the widow of Thomas Greenleaf. These newspapers were vehement Republican organs, sharply critical of the Federalist administration and were the instruments for the opinions of Thomas Jefferson, Aaron Burr, and other Anti-Federalists in New York City.

On November 6, 1799, the following item was published in the *Argus*.

Extract of a letter from Philadelphia
dated September 20.

An effort was recently made to suppress the AURORA, and
Alexander Hamilton was at the bottom of it. Mrs. Bache was
offered 6,000 dollars down, in the presence of several persons,
in part payment; the valuation to be left to two impartial persons, and the remainder paid immediately on her giving up the
paper; but she pointedly refused it, and declared she would not
dishonor her husband's memory, nor her children's future fame
by such baseness. When she parted with the paper, it would be
to republicans only. 'I am proud to hear of your honourable
state's republicanism. The change in men's minds here is truly
astonishing.'

It would not be amiss to enquire by what magic Mr. Hamilton
finds it in his power to raise the sum of money to spare, sufficient to purchase the Aurora, the establishment of which is
worth between 15 and 20,000 dollars. In order to do away a
charge of speculation brought against him while he was Secretary of the Treasury, he says he was not able to raise 1,000 dollars at one time— —. To support this assertion, he brings forward the receipts of James Reynolds, the reputed husband of
the dear Maria, for that sum paid him at different periods;
alleging that a Secretary of the Treasury who had been guilty
of the crime laid to his charge, could not possibly be supposed
to require time for the payment of so small a sum, when the de-
lay left it in the power of Reynolds to blast his character. If the
quondam Secretary was really as poor as he wished to make us
believe, how happens it that he can now throw away thou-
sands upon an object that was to bring him in nothing. Perhaps
however, the money was to be raised in the same manner that
Callender was to be driven out of Richmond—by an association
of orderly federalists. There is also another resource—British
secret service money— a hint to Sir Robert would do the business at once. Mr. Liston is so well bred a man, that he could not
politely refuse to enter into the plan. By becoming a partner
in the concern he would naturally expect to screen the "Defen-
der of the Faith," and his satellites from many *hard rubs* which
the *mildness* of the sedition law as yet suffers the Aurora to bestow on them; and also prevent his courtly ears from being
offended with the repetition of the story of the horse thief
dispatches, British influences, &c. One would have supposed that

Mr. Hamilton might have fallen upon a better plan to suppress the Aurora; for it is a bungling piece of work at best, to attempt to suppress a paper by putting it in the power of the proprietors, to furnish themselves with a new set of materials. We would advise him, as he is now a major general, to call on Capt. Montgomery, and his troop, whose heroism in the Northampton expedition certainly entitles them to this post of *honor*—they might have gibbetted the Editor and destroyed the office so effectively in half an hour, that not a vestige would have remained. This would have been attended with no expense whatever, which to a *poor man* as the general *was*, should be matter of serious consideration. It is astonishing that this did not occur to him— Nothing should have escaped a man of such *nice calculations*.[42]

On November 9, 1799, David Frothingham was arrested on the complaint of Alexander Hamilton for violation of the Alien and Sedition Laws.* The following excerpt from the eulogistic study of Alexander Hamilton by Henry Cabot Lodge reveals Hamilton's written views on the reasons for his complaint against David Frothingham:

A little later in the same year 1799, and in a similar spirit, he wrote to ask the Attorney-General, Hoffman, to prosecute a newspaper, which has charged him with suppressing the "Aurora" by pecuniary means.

'Hitherto', he says, 'I have foreborne to resort to the laws for the authors or abettors (of such attacks) and were I to

---

*"The Alien and Sedition Acts of 1798 were directed against foreign-born Republican editors and others who were notorious in their vituperative attacks on the leaders of the government. Obviously partisan laws sponsored by the Federalists they expired with the Adams administration in 1801.
Few country printers were prosecuted under these laws as they were intended for bigger game, the editors of such leading Republican papers as the Philadelphia *Aurora*, the New York *Argus*, etc."[43]

consult personal considerations alone, I should continue in this
course, paying hatred with contempt. But public motives now
compel me to a different conduct. The designs of that faction
to overthrow our government,* and with it the great pillars of
social security and happiness in this country, become every day
more manifest, and have of late acquired a system that renders
them formidable.'

He now adds that one engine for the destruction of society
is the issue of libels calculated to destroy the character of the
most 'conspicuous supporters of the government, as, in this instance, by charging them with attempts to stifle the liberty of
the press;" and he says that "these intrigues and calumnies are
carried on by American citizens aided by foreign gold."[45]

Though neither the *Argus* nor David Frothingham were mentioned specifically by Lodge or
Hamilton there can be no doubt that this letter
by Hamilton referred directly to them. Frothingham's arrest and trial were the only recorded
complaints made by Hamilton at that time with
regard to "the suppression of the *Aurora* by
pecuniary means."

The events of the arrest and trial were given
front page coverage in *Greenleaf's New York
Journal and Partriotic Register* and, interesting to
note, were written in the usual partisan style of
the day. The minutes of the trial were printed
verbatim, and the editorial comment was un-
sparing in its abuse of Hamilton and what he represented. The trial was another opportunity for

*Wandell in his study of Aaron Burr suggested that Aaron
Burr had been rumored to have had plans to separate New Enland from the Union. It is possible that the rumors may have
originated through channels such as the above letter.[44]

the Republican press to hammer away at their opponents. With the issue of freedom of the press at stake, and with the fact that Frothingham was being punished for a reprint of a letter that he did not compose, and where the original printer was not punished, the press had a field day. The trial provided strong campaign propaganda needed to win the Presidential election of the coming year, and the most was made of it.

Hamilton may have had yet another problem at the time of the publication of the letter in the *Argus*. The tragic loss of life caused by the yellow fever epidemic had aided Aaron Burr in accomplishing a shrewd political maneuver. He had succeeded in obtaining swift passage of a Bill in the New York State Legislature "for supplying the City of New York with pure and wholesome water." The Water Bill became a law on April 2, 1799. One clause of this law stated that "the surplus capital might be employed in any way not inconsistent with the laws and Constitution of the United States or of the State of New York." Consequently, under the terms of a law to establish a better water system for New York City, Aaron Burr used the extra available funds to form the Bank of Manhattan. Heretofore, the only banks in New York City were the Bank of New York, which was controlled by Alexander Hamilton, and a branch of the Bank of the United States.* Burr's plan to open another bank in competition and the method by which this was accomplished, no doubt, was a source of extreme irritation to Hamilton. The very same pages of *Greenleaf's New York Journal and Patriotic Register* that gave detailed accounts of the trial contained the legal notices announcing the establishment of the Bank of Manhattan. It is possible that the interest in the trial served Burr's purposes very well in luring the inquiry away from the details of the founding of his bank.

On November 13, 1799, *Greenleaf's New York Journal and Patriotic Register* reported the following:

On Saturday, last, Mr. David Frothingham was arrested at the suit of the *chaste* Alexander Hamilton, for publishing in the Argus of the 6th inst., an extract of a letter from Philadelphia, which extract, was inserted in several papers, in various parts of the Union, prior to its appearance in the Argus. Bail was given for Mr. Frothingham's appearance at court the first week in next month.[48]

Elsewhere in the same paper was printed:

Wednesday, November 13
Notice was served yesterday that the trial of David Frothingham for a publication which appeared in this paper last Tuesday would take place this day.[49]

The following week, the following editorial appeared in *Greenleaf's New York Journal and Patriotic Register* :

---

*These two banks were both under Federalist control. "The Federalists . . . disposed of sufficient power at Albany to prevent the granting of any rival charters."[47]

Wednesday, November 20, 1799

The trial of David Frothingham, belonging to the office of the *Argus*, for copying in our paper of the 6th, a publication which previously appeared in several other prints, 'stating that an attempt had been made to purchase the establishment of the AURORA, and that Alexander Hamilton was at the bottom of it.', takes place this day before the Supreme Court. It has been a matter of surprise to many persons that this nonpareil of chastity should wave prosecuting the author of this extract, or taking any measures to discover him, but should make the *Argus* the butt of his revenge. To us it is no way astonishing—we know the man and had his conduct been more extraordinary, our wonder would not have been more excited. That he should be an enemy to the *Argus* is quite confident, that he should lie in wait for an occasion to harass it, although in the possession of the relic of its own late proprietor is worthy of a man, whose deeds have been registered with its own hand. The press has often exposed intrigues, and produced discoveries beneficial to the public interests. Had it not been for the press, the 'strict morality,' and the undeviating virtue of this gentleman, would he have ever arrived to that degree of celebrity which he has attained. A hypocrite generally boasts of his merit and his good deed in public. He appears to meritorious acts merely for the purpose of exciting applause and not for the gratification of self-approbation. Such a character is perhaps odious to the General, and it is very likely, his ire has been provoked against the press for publishing to the world, what a good friend he has been to female distress; how like the angel of charity, he has poured the balm of consolation on a poverty struck matron; that he deigned to stoop from his then high and important station, to console the sorrows and to relieve the woes of an afflicted fair one. That even his purse strings were drawn to bestow pecuniary aid to him that ought to have been her real guardian. That publication of all this was a drawback upon that internal satisfaction, which he enjoyed in private. He perhaps conceived that the notoriety of his charitable actions diminished much of their merit, and that there might be men unjustly suspicious of his having prompted the publicity of his benevolent conduct. The press has been impudently officious in blazoning forth the amiablity of the man. He has been incensed at its interference and has embraced the first opportunity to prove his enmity of it.[50]

The occasion of Frothingham's arrest and trial dutifully reported by the sister newspaper of the *Argus*, became an excellent opportunity to expound with relish upon the character of the political enemy. The editorial of *Greenleaf's New York Journal and Patriotic Register* on December 7, 1799, again took up the cause for David Frothingham in its introductory sentences, but this time, jumped quickly from there to the principles of freedom of the press:

The trial of Mr. David Frothingham is preparing for the press, and will appear in a few days. Our fellow citizens cannot but feel for the situation of a man, who was in no way bound to be responsible for any publication of this paper, had he not from the most generous motives placed himself between the proprietor and prosecution. Never, we believe, has his case been paralleled. Never has a journeyman-printer been prosecuted for anything appearing in a paper. It has been most unjustly reported that the extract of a letter, for which this man suffers, originated with us, and was first published in the *Argus*. In order, therefore, to prove to the most ignorant Federalist the falsity of this assertion, and to point out the generosity of their champion, we shall just state the facts. It first appeared about the 1st of October last in the '*Epitome of the Times*,' a paper published in Norfolk, some time after in the '*Constitutional Telegraph*,' a Boston paper, and in the '*Centinal of Freedom*', published at Newark, Thus was it published in three different papers, in different parts of the continent, before it was copied unto the *Argus*. The anger of 'a man of many works,' slept until the *Argus* repeated what he terms a libel. Like the Roman who pretended slumber, while his spouse entertained guests; but perceiving one day a man whom he disliked, was about to be admitted to the same freedoms, he suddenly awoke, and cried out, 'non dormio amaibus, I sleep not for all,' So the 'guardian of the marriage bed' overlooked the author, and remained quiet until the *Argus* copied the 'Publication.' Then and not till then, did this 'chaste supporter' of 'public security and private happiness,' feel enraged. Forth came his flaming epistle, depicting the wickedness of the faction opposed to him, and frought with the most delicate informations of his own worth and virtue. Too long he asserted that he has taken the subject of calumny, and that it is now time to put a stop to it. Much, we acknowledge, has been said of his conduct. Whether he thinks that any reference to his exploits in the field of Mars, or in that of Venus, is a calmuny or not, we shall leave it to others to decide. If the dangerous opinion of Lord Mansfield that 'the greater the truth, the greater the libel,' is a maxim with him, then, indeed, we ought to wave any examination into the nature of calumny. The case of Cooney, the printer of the Morning Post, in Dublin, has been spoken of as forming a precedent for this prosecution. Cooney was tried and found guilty for publishing a libel against the Queen, which was copied from a London print, and was passed unnoticed by the English Attorney General. But are we to go to Ireland for precedents where law, justice, and right, have to be sported with, and known only as exploded terms. Where corruption, perjury, and veniality kicks the mean accursed tyrants. In England, the press enjoys a liberty, which the Irish press has been totally deprived of. The British government in Ireland did by force and violence destroy offices and printing materials, of those papers, which exercised the freedom of opinion. Not satisfied with harassing the printers, with persecutions, fines and imprisonment, they robbed them of their property at noon day.[51]

The trial was reported by *Greenleaf's New York Journal and Patriotic Register* in their issue of December 11, 1799:

Trial of David Frothingham, for LIBEL against
Gen. Alexander Hamilton.

On Thursday, 21st, November, 1799, case on the Court of Oyer and Terminer, in this city, the Trial of DAVID FROTHING-HAM, for a Libel against Alexander Hamilton, Esquire, a major general in the service of the United States——
The judges who presided at the trial were
His Honour, Mr. Justice Radcliffe,
The Hon. Richard Varick, Mayor of the City; and
The Hon. Richard Harrison, Recorder of the City.

The publication which gave rise to the indictment as copied in the *Argus* of the 6th inst., from the *Constitutional Telegraph* is as follows:

Copy of the extract of a letter from Philadelphia
date September 20.

Defendant pleaded not guilty

Mr. Colden, Assistant District Attorney, received a letter from Alexander Hamilton, directing the present prosecution. He spoke to Mrs. Greenleaf who claimed she knew nothing about it. They went to David Frothingham, and after conversation with him decided that David Frothingham was liable. Alexander Hamilton was offered as a witness to prove falsity of the publication. Mr. Brockholst Livingston, counsel for the defence, objected that that was not the issue——The Court after deciding that the truth of a libel could not be given in evidence but they considered him a competent witness to prove other points.'Mr.Hamilton testified that he had never been concerned in making an offer to Mrs. Bache for the purchase of the *Aurora* and then gave an history of the speculation which he had been charged, while Secretary of the Treasury and of the mode he had pursued to disprove this accusation. Also, that he considered the *Aurora* as a paper hostile to the government of the United States'. . . Mr. Livingston then offered to prove that the defendant was neither the Editor nor the Proprietor of the *Argus*, nor a sharer in the profits, by producing the receipt book of Mrs. Greenleaf, which would show that he had only been a journeyman-printer in her office, at a salary of 8 dollars per week, He offered to call witnesses to prove the agreement between the defendant and Mrs. Greenleaf. The Attorney General objected because he claimed the defendant had confessed himself the publisher, and thereby assumed all responsibility on himself. Mr. Livingston said when the manner and the circumstances of the defendant's confession were considered, it amounted to but little. It appeared to him rather like a piece of gallantry, calculated to screen a woman from prosecution, than resulting from a conviction of his own guilt. 'A man cannot substitute himself in the place of another in a criminal case.' The court refused to receive any testimony to show who were the Proprietor or Editor of the *Argus*, or in what capacity the defendant lived with Mrs. Greenleaf. Mr. Livingston offered to

show that the publication had appeared in other papers before
it was copied. This was also overruled.

The arguments for the defense were: 1. There was no libel,
2. David Frothingham had no liability. 'If the *Aurora* was really
hostile to the government, it would really be a meritorious act
on the part of Mr. Hamilton to suppress it through purchase,'
remarked Brockholst Livingston, counsel for the defence. Mr.
Livingston said he was willing to meet the Attorney-General
fairly and admitted for the sake of argument that the author
had declared Mr. Hamilton not to be a republican.—If by this
we mean that Mr. Hamilton was not a republican in sentiment.
Mr. Livingston could see nothing serious in this accusation. 'As
long as any one was obedient to the laws and a good subject it
was not necessary that he should think the form of government
under which he lived the best of all possible forms. He might
think a limited monarchy, or any other constitution of government better. He might think a monarchy more stable, less
liable to change, and holding forth greater security to personal
liberty and property than a democratic or republican government . . . Even as a public man, he might propose an amendment to the constitution declaring that the office of the President should be hereditary; and that the title of the first magis-
trate should be changed to that of a king.[52]

Judge Radcliffe, in his charge to the jury, felt
there was not a shadow of a doubt in his mind
that the letter was libelous and that the defendant was "answerable" for it. The jury brought
in the verdict of "guilty" in about three hours.

Mr. Livingston pleaded for mitigation of
punishment for his client:

. . . to the effect that he was not the Editor or the Proprietor of
the *Argus*, and gets no profit from it, that he received from Mrs.
Anne Greenleaf, 8 dollars per week. That the publication was reprinted from other papers before it was in the *Argus*. That he
didn't know who wrote the letter which he did not consider

libel on General Hamilton or any other person. That the deponent has a wife, and six small children, the eldest of whom is
12 years of age, and all reside on the East end of Long Island,
that the deponent has no other means, whatever, of supporting
his wife, family, and himself, but the weekly salary of 8 dollars.[53]

The Attorney General offered a counter plea
for no mercy, inasmuch as subsequent issues of
the *Argus* after November 6 continued to reflect
on the character of General Hamilton. Mr. Livingston disagreed with this argument.

"Since Frothingham was neither the Editor nor Proprietor
of the later issues he wasn't responsible for any but the first.
If the defendant was liable for the posterior publications, he
might be indicted for them, and thus be punished for the same
offense.[54]

David Frothingham then offered a letter of
complete denial of ever having written "a single
line for or against Alexander Hamilton since
November 6th, 1799, and whoever wrote them
he doesn't know."[55]

"The Judge in passing sentence, observed that, if the defendant
was poor, he should have thought of that before he committed
the offense, that his poverty was no reason for mitigating his
punishment."[55]

An excerpt from *Greenleaf's New York Journal and Patriotic Register* of December 7, 1799,
stated:

Yesterday, Mr. David Frothingham, Foreman in the Office
of the *Argus*, was sentenced to pay a fine of One Hundred Dollars, and to be confined for Four Months in the Bridewell, for
copying a publication into this paper, reflecting upon the Amor-

ous General Hamilton. Be it remembered that the Jury* recommended Frothingham to the mercy of the Court. How kindly has it complied.

The Jury, with but few exceptions, were known to be all Federalists, as also were the Judges.[57]

This phase of Frothingham's life is quite clear. He was given a comparatively severe sentence following his arrest on the complaint of Alexander Hamilton for libel under the terms of

---

*"A search has been made of the records of the Court of General Sessions and I enclose herewith an extract of the minutes of the court . . . I thought you would be interested in the names of the Jurors who sat in the trial" [Excerpt from letter from Office of District Attorney, Thomas E. Dewey of New York City, August 18, 1939.]

Thursday, 11 A.M. Nov. 21, 1799
Benjamin Thurston, William Franklin
Adam Nestell, James Hallett
Andrew Lewis, Francis Cooper
Leonard Lispenard, Frederick Lintz
David Adee, Jacob Frost
John Wilson, Philip Rhinelander
Found Guilty, Tuesday 11 A.M. Dec. 3, 1799
People *vs* David Frothingham
A verdict of Conviction on an indictment for a Libel on Alexander Hamilton, Esquire.
IT IS CONSIDERED AND ADJURED by the court here that the said David Frothingham the aforesaid defendant be for the said offence whereof he is convicted pay a fine of One Hundred dollars and that he be imprisoned in the Bridewell of the City of New York for the term of Four Calendar Months.
AND IT IS FURTHER ORDERED that he stand committed until the said Fine is paid, and until he enter into Recognizance himself in One Thousand dollars or One Competent Surety in the sum of one thousand dollars Conditioned for the good Behavior of the defendant for the term of two years after the expiration of said imprisonment."[58]

the Alien and Sedition Laws. The whole matter
is rather confused. First, it was a common practice of the time to reprint articles from other
newspapers. The letter in question was neither
written by Frothingham nor originally printed in
the *Argus*. No attempt seemed to have been
made by the prosecution to seek out the author
of the letter. Second, Frothingham was only an
employee, and it was not his responsibility in any
case. The liability for the libel should have included Mrs. Greenleaf as well as the newspaper in
which the letter originated since such was mentioned in the complaint. This was not done.

It should be noted that Brockholst Livingston
was Frothingham's attorney, and the arguments
during the trial were political. Livingston used
the contents of the letter to emphasize Hamilton's political views. Brockholst Livingston
was one of Aaron Burr's political henchmen. He
was a member of the powerful Livingston clan
who were concerned with political control of New
York State. His alignment with Aaron Burr concentrated on the defeat of the politically powerful
Federalists—the Schuylers—into whose family,
Alexander Hamilton had married. Brockholst
Livingston was a wealthy and influential man,
and one whom David Frothingham could never
possibly afford to employ for his defense. That
he pleaded the case for David Frothingham, and
that he pleaded the case in the manner he did,

would lead to the conclusion that Frothingham
was just a figurehead in the trial against Alexander Hamilton.   It was rather a battle between
Alexander Hamilton and the Republicans. It may
be further concluded that Mr. Hamilton felt that
by punishing Frothingham he might intimidate
Aaron Burr who was growing much too powerful
and popular in the New York area. Perhaps this
action against David Frothingham might frighten
the publishing organs of the Republicans into
stifling their explosive attacks on the Federalists.
The trial of David Frothingham, a relatively in-
significant journeyman-printer, on the charge of
libel for something he did not write, in a paper he
did not own, that had been printed and reprinted
previously, is an indication of the anxiety caused
by the concerted attacks of the Republican press.
The list of names of the judge and the jury further indicates the weight of the Federalists' hand.
Frothingham was a warning, a threat, and an example to those who were becoming too bold.

The legal prosecution of Frothingham did not
end the vengeance wrought upon him by the Federalists. After he was imprisoned at Bridewell,
he was never heard from again. From this point
there are only theories as to what happened to
him with no records to substantiate them. One
theory is that he was sent out West with other
political prisoners and killed. There is an unveri-
fied statement in Wyman that Frothingham

died up the Congo River in Africa on October 8, 1822. His tombstone at Sag Harbor marks his date of death as 1814. This date was determined following an item in a Boston newspaper that one David Frothingham was on a boat which sank at sea. Which theory is correct is not known, nor is it known whether any of these theories are correct. All that is known for certain is that upon his admission to Bridewell, he disappeared and was apparently never heard from again.

On Saturday, December 25, 1799, the following advertisement was printed in *Greenleaf's New York Journal and Patriotic Register*: "A Foreman of Respectability, wanted at the office of the *Argus*."[59]

PART III *Chapter Six*
ANALYSIS OF FROTHINGHAM'S
LONG ISLAND HERALD

IN VOLUME 1, NO. 1 OF *Frothingham's Long Island Herald,*, dated May 10, 1791, Frothingham
promised by means of his open letter to the public "to render this paper a useful repository of
knowledge, humour and entertainment," and
sought to "expand the mind and embelish the
understanding." He added that "every branch
of literature will be ransacked" and "a corner will
be devoted to the treasure of those in the poetic
line."[60]

His motto, "Eye Nature's Walks, Shoot Folly
as it Flies, — And Catch the Manners Living
as they Rise," can be construed to corroborate his
expressed ideal for the proper standards of a good
newspaper: truth and impartiality. This claim
for truth and impartiality in his newspaper was
reiterated again and again by Frothingham. On
September 20, 1797, he wrote:

We dispense retailing such idle reports and foolish stories about
a man who spoke to another, who spoke to a third, who told a
fourth, that a fifth saw a Captain who spoke to a British packet,
and got information of a Place, &c., &c., such nonsensical
trumpery shall never disgrace the impartial pages of the Herald
. . . It must be the sincere desire and ardent wish of every one
that so laudable and praiseworthy an undertaking may meet
with encouragement tantamount to its merits.[61]

On July 23, 1798, the following article appeared:

Aware of the difficulty of affording GENERAL satisfaction
especially at times, when the public mind is agitated in the manner it has been for twelve months past, the Editor is apprehen-
sive that he may have displeased some, and that he may have
been hastily charged with professing UNJUSTIFIABLE
PRINCIPLES. But he trusts that a recurrence to the several
numbers of the Herald will prove he never deviated from "IM-
PARTIALITY" — the brightest ornament of the Press.[62]

"Vice, the bane of society, with its concomitant attendants, will be branded with every mark
of infamy." These words of promise were also
included in his opening letter that established
his editorial policy. Accordingly each issue contained some elaborations on the blessings of virtue versus the dangers of sin. For instance, a random review of the subjects covered included a
Dissertation of Drunkenness, on Singularity of
Manners, a poem on Friendship, an essay on
Courage, one on Hope, and another on Revenge,
a poem to the Ladies on Proper Dress, an article
on Common Sense in Dishabille, and a Warning
to Coquets, [sic] as well as many lessons on slander and jealousy.

It is immediately apparent to the reader that
the *Herald* was a political sheet with little or no
local news except for notices of local elections and
political meetings. Like other country newspapers the printed material dealt with the affairs of
governments, of Congress, of state and Federal

officials, foreign wars, and elections. Probably there was no need to repeat the neighborhood gossip as that spread quickly enough by word of mouth and would be old news by the time it was read in print. The subscribers expected information of the world outside and the newspaper with its report of the national and world developments was their contact of communication.

The news items in *Frothingham's Long Island Herald*, both foreign and domestic, were primarily reprinted from other newspapers, and there is no doubt that the subscribers to this paper were concerned about affairs of the government, federal, state and county, as well as foreign affairs. Since the news was clipped from other newspapers, the printer was the one to determine the reading fare of his public, and he was in a position to feed material he thought important and of interest to his readers. If **he** had an axe to grind, or if he was under the influence of others who directed him to grind their axe, it was simple enough to print only material which suited his purpose. If the subscribers to the paper were satisfied with what they read, they were free agents to purchase the paper. The subscriber was not captive and could discontinue his paper if he was dissatisfied with the printer's political views or choice of materials. Of course, it must be remembered that oftimes because of limited communications the reader of the country newspaper was not always aware that the news excerpts had been slanted to a particular point of view and he undoubtedly accepted what he read at its face value.

Frothingham, as has been noted, kept reminding his readers of his "impartiality" in presentation of the news and shared with them his untiring efforts in this regard. On September 20, 1797, he again informed the public of this fact:

We have selected the most important articles from the late papers received for this day's Herald—What we communicate is chiefly from arrivals at the Southward &c. Some information and such entertainment may be found upon a careful perusal. Arrivals from Europe are momently expected, and undoubtedly matters of importance are now floating on Old Ocean . . . Each week the freshest intelligence from the southern and westward papers will be transplanted into the pages of the Herald; and by extracting the most important and loping off the superfluous branches, we shall be able to garnish our pages with the most essential upon every subject.[63]

On reading through the pages of the *Herald* from the early issues of the paper to its later ones, it becomes evident that a change in editorial policy had taken place. The early issues concerned themselves with legal, maritime, literary material, and favored France, and the cause of Liberty but in a mild and innocuous fashion. However, the *Herald*, during its last two years, presented an entirely different picture. It had become more and more outspokenly partisan. It was more and more daring in its attacks on the government, the Federalists, England, and other printers and newspapers of Federalist sympathies. Swept along in an increasing wave of un-controlled anger and vehemence so prevalent among the party presses of that time, the *Herald* pursued a relentless program for the defeat of the Federalists at home and for peace with France abroad. No holds were barred as the *Herald* joined the free-for-all in its determination to mold public opinion in its favor.

Some excerpts from the *Herald* may serve to illustrate the nature and flavor of its political material. The following represented a quiet, reasonable, and dignified criticism of the government:

Several very worthy men have been alarmed into places of great trust and emolument.

The Constitution has been personified in eight or ten men who know not what it means and who have altered it so that scarcely any person can know it.

The emoluments of the church are mistaken for religion, and the income of a pensioner is called property.

The reformation of abuses is seditious &c. treasonable, and nothing is wrong which can be proved to be old.

Indemnity consists in surrendering all we have taken, and security is synonymous with implicit confidence in those who have deceived us.[64]

Antipathy for England was demonstrated by the *Herald* in many ways; ridicule was just one of them:

On the Three-Cornered Hat—

Among the many things invented by man, . . . none perhaps is more ridiculous than the three-cornered hat at present used by some persons . . . Common sense points out their inconsistency, and reason mocks the stupidity of him who made submits to be ruled by custom, that tyrant of the human mind, to the whole government three-fourths of this creation foolishly subscribe their assent.[65]

On May 24, 1797, all of page two and part of page three of the *Herald* were devoted to a verbatim reprint of the President's speech on the situation with France. The following week the newspaper contained an editorial reprint from a New York newspaper recommending that Jefferson or Madison be sent to France to try to come to amicable agreement between France and the United States.

. . . The right of declaring War is vested in Congress. The President's Phillipic against France, therefore only throws the zeal against that Republic; but the ultimate decision is exclusive in Congress. He may recommend, but that is all. He has no voice, or vote in the question, or mode of declaring war, and if he attempts to negotiate the country into hostilities against any nation, he is responsible for the consequence. A declaration of war is a legislative act, it is not therefore to be submitted to Presidential inspection. He is simply to execute National will; But it does not appear that he has any right to influence that will. Let us wait therefore in patience, relying on the only constitutional authority deposited by the people in congress, no doubt to guard against personal prejudices and passion, to save our country from a war with the Republic of France which would indeed be our destroying angel.[66]

On June 21, 1797, the following reprint from *Greenleaf's New York Journal and Patriotic Register* of a letter "To the PEOPLE OF AMERICA" appeared on the front page of the *Herald*:

To exhibit to the public a few Stricture on the present status of Politics so far as they concern the honor and interest of the U. S., may appear as necessary as at any period since the establishment of the American empire—and perhaps, it may be equally important at this alarming crisis, to state with candor, the usage of our government to the several powers at war, with whom we have any political relation, of commercial concern.

... The whole world has witnessed two of the greatest revolutions that any generation ever produced—and the same evidences are at liberty to declare whether Washington's administration had paid to France the debt of gratitude which they owe her.

We do not justify France in her depredations of our commerce, but if a certain party could justify the British adjudication system, upon the grounds the ruin of France was her main object, surely candour alone will justify France upon a more liberal basis;——

But while our executive and twenty chosen men feel so strong a propensity to form treaties with foreign nations ... those who impose such an idea are political impostors.

... What then are our prospects of war with France, nothing but ruin and disgrace. People of America—avoid political broils with foreign nations: let prudence direct, and wisdom govern your public councils: Let the idea of war vanish: adhere to the cultivation of domestic tranquility.   JUNO

Our country certainly has never been since the close of the American War in so precarious a situation as it is at the present period ... JUNIUS[67]

In the same issue, on page three, there was an excerpt reprinted from a Baltimore paper:

Little do we know the arts that have been practiced to embroil the people of the United States with the French Revolution.[68]

Another reprint from *Greenleaf's New York Journal and Patriotic Register* was included the following week:

To the people of America
I call upon you, O people of America, First born in the family
of Freeman to exert your right in this awful crisis of approach-
ing calamity . . . Rally round the standard of your Independence . . . preserve by every effort the inestimable blessings of
Peace. JUNO[69]

Here was an attempt at political satire:

Political Conundrum: Why is Federalism like
Charity? Because it covers a 'multitude of sins.'[70]

What motivated Frothingham in his vehement
attacks on the government, on England, and on
the opposing press? It can only be conjectured,
as there are no records available. It is known
that there was sickness in his family, as noted in
the issue of April 12, 1797: "The Deficiency of
our last week's paper, was owing to sickness in
our family . . ."[71] Furthermore, there is written
evidence of a need for money when his press and
office were mortgaged to Messrs. Dering, Hodges
and Fordham on February 1, 1797.[72] Could
these men have exercised some control over the
editorial policy of the *Herald*?

With the stage distributing the *Herald*
throughout the Island, and with the subscribers
in New York City, the *Herald* was in competition
with the city newspapers. Perhaps Frothingham
did not object too much if his patrons pressed
him to take a more relentless stand. Perhaps he
had visions of taking a place next to such great

newspaper publishers as Benjamin Franklin
Bache of the Philadelphia *Aurora* or Philip Freneau of the *National Gazette* both of whom were
leading newspaper spokesmen for Thomas Jefferson and James Madison. In his impoverished
state in 1797, with a wife and six children to support, he may have taken the giant step forward
in his journalistic tactics in the hope of attract-
ing the attention of one of the political conten-
ders of the period. It is even possible that he had
already been approached by the leading Republicans of the period. There are no records to
substantiate these suppositions, it is true, but
one thing is certain, the *Herald* had become a
fighting political organ, and despite Frothingham's repeated protests of "impartiality," the
paper seemed to be dedicated to one purpose:
to disparage, to expose, and to humilate the Federalist party and to bring about its downfall.

Moreover, Frothingham's Republican newspaper, not content with its campaign against the
Federalists, Anglophiles, and Francophobes, also
began to bear down with concentrated vigor on
the Federalist printing presses and their printers.
On August 9, 1797, he reported the following
item to his readers:

The Philadelphia Porcupine with its accustomed venom has
been shooting at our distinguished representative in Congress.
But like the viper that bites a file, vain are his attempts to
wound.[73]

This evidence of standard journalistic camaradie between fellow printers appeared in the *Herald* on June 25, 1797:

From Porcupine's Gazette
A man by the name of DAVID FROTHINGHAM who publishes a vile Sans Culotte paper called the LONG ISLAND HERALD, sent me his paper, and written on it. 'Send me, if you please, yours, once in a while.' I will never send him one, and I hereby order him to send me no more of his. It is impregnated with such poisonous matter that I should be afraid to taste a fowl tinged with it.[74]

Beneath the reprint from *Porcupine's Gazette*, in the same issue, Frothingham printed his answer to his brother journalist:

'His tongue is the tongue of slander, the poison of Asps issues from his lips.'
To give our Readers an idea of the writer of the above paragraph, we should inform them that he is a Billingsgate Scoundrel, transported to this country by Will Pitt, and his party.
His real name is William Cobbett, he publishes a daily newspaper in the city of Philadelphia, his only support is Englishmen, Tories, and Refugees. Each morning is issued through his 'stink-pot of Sedition,' the most scandalous and abusive epithets against public men and measures—and private characteristics attacked with the most scurrilous language. Not long since, his Foxy Scalp, received a just battering with true American Hickory, for a libelous, low, livid pun upon a gentleman of known Republican principles and respectability in Philadelphia.
It is not to be wondered at that an exchange of papers had not taken place, as the least paragraph that favors on true Republicanism knaws upon his callow soul, like aquesortus upon iron.
Ever since this 'Skunk' opened his pandorus box upon the city of Philadelphia, it has been yearly visited an epidemic disease, and no wonder, when they allow such vile contaminating miserants to eat the bread and breathe the air of REPUBLICANS.[75]

And, as if Frothingham were not satisfied with his answer to his enemy of the press, he persisted in the battle and on September 27, 1797, came back again with another denunciation:

Time Piece of Capt. Freneau 'unrivalled in excellence by any paper in New York.'
  It has been attacked without any provocation by Mr. Fenno and that Billingsgate hero Porcupine who never extracted an article from it without accompanying it with his usual wholesale manner with six times as much abuse.

> From Penn's famous city what hoasts have departed
> The Streets and the houses are nearly deserted,
> But still their remain
> Two Vipers, that's plain,
> Who soon it is thought, yellow flag will display;
> Old Porcupine preaching
> And Fenno beseeching
> Some dung-cart to wheel him away.[76]

Frothingham's Long Island Herald was not entirely political in its content. Interspersed among the news items were other items of popular interest.   Consequently, these words of good cheer from a letter from Philadelphia were to be found in the issue of September 13, 1797, at the time when a severe yellow fever epidemic was raging: "Cure for yellow fever. Bread and molasses and gin-grog — Cure within two hours."[77]   In the same vein of popular interest, and in the same issue of the *Herald*, a cure was offered for another current problem: "Dysentery — Take Marshmallows,* boil leaves and stalks in water

---

*It must be noted that the marshmallows cited were a type of medicinal herb.

till you reduce the liquid one half. Pour it off and drink half a pint at a time, and as often as may be agreeable."[78]

The advertisements in the *Herald* were most revealing about the social life and customs of that period:

1) Ran away from the Subscriber an indented Girl, by the name of Temperance, white. Whoever will take up said Girl and bring her to the Subscriber shall receive TWO CENTS reward ... [79]
2) [Samuel Ward wants a] Smart, active Lad, about 13 or 14 years of age as an apprentice to the Turnplate working and Coppersmith Business.[80]
3) [Henry Parsons found] a middling size SKIFF painted red.[81]
4) [Twenty dollars reward offered by Samuel C. Carmans.] Sat. May 6. Negrow man named ARTER, 28 years, 5'10". He has 2 scars, one on each foot, from the end of his toes almost up to his ankles.[82] [As of the issue of June 21, 1797, ARTER was still missing.][83]
5) ... A beautiful assortment of European and India GOODS... will be sold very cheap for cash.[84]

No doubt, the Sag Harbor version of the modern department store was the firm of Dering, Fordham, and Hodges who had "on sale at their store ... on the most reasonable terms," the following:

Cloths of different kinds and colors including Ruffils and Ruffilets, muslin, Bed Ticking and Check lining, Flannels, serges, Veil shapes, handkerchiefs of Jaconet, Muslin, Barcelona, Bandano and polecat, Dutch English, a Double Bottle Powder, Best English Glue, Oil Vitriol by the lb. or larger quantity and as cheap as can be purchased in New-York; Wool cards by the Doz. or single pear, Hollow Ware of all kinds, Drugs, Medicines of many kinds, Crockery and Glass Ware, 6x8 and 7x9 Window Glass, Brandy, spirits or Country Rum by the Barrel or less

quantity, Coffee and Chocolate, Powder and Shott, Rice and
Indigo, Snuff by the Bladder &c., Stove lime by the cask . . . [85]

The largest proportion of advertising for the
individual was done by the Printer himself, advertising the products of his press, his bookshop,
his bindery, and his stationery store, as well as
his calls for rags, hog's bristles, goose quills,
sheepskins, and other related material necessary for him to perform his printing and book-
binding operations.

1) [The Printer asked for] 40 weight of live geese feathers.[86]
2) [The Printer asked for] a few tons of good English hay.[87]
3) Wanted immediately by Printing Office. Green Sheepskins
for which price will be given according to their goodness.[88]

The literary offerings from his book shop, as
determined through his advertisements, reveal
the reading tastes of the period. Among the most
popular class of reading were religious books and
sermons. It was a regular practice for sermons of
local ministers to be printed and sold. Almost
every issue of the *Herald* advertised in one form
or another that copies of sermons might be
obtained at the Printing Office.

If there was one book to which the farmers
were sure to subscribe, that book was the almanac. An advertisement in the December 13, 1791
issue of the *Herald* enumerated the contents of
the Almanack for 1792:

This day is Published to be sold at the Printing Office at Sag
Harbor, 6 pence single or 3 shillings per doz.
The U. S. Almanack for Year of Our Lord, 1792.

Containing
Besides what is usual in an Almanack
Stages in Life
The Atheist, an odd Story
On Matrimony
The Devil Killed by a Shepherd
Why a Blockhead generally succeeds better in business
    than a Man of Wit
An excellent example of frugality
The Arcana of Physic
Anectode of Gen Gates.
A beautiful ejaculation to Health
Three Passions should be governed by Reason
The Religion of Libertines
Anecdote of Benjamin Lay
Equinox
Maxim
Courts of the United States
Friends of yearly meetings
Supreme Courts of this State
Census of the United States
A table of Interest
Governors of the different States
Patriotism
Table of the Coins of the United States
A Table of Discount per Cent
A List of Roads
Maxims, &c.[89]

Since many homes contained no other literature but the Almanac it can readily be seen that
the readers of the Almanac had quite a choice of
reading matter. This Almanack of 1792 was
probably not printed by Frothingham's press
though the advertisment could be interpreted to
indicate that it was."*

*McMurtrie noted in his study of the Sag Harbor imprints
of David Frothingham: "There is no evidence that any local Sag
Harbor almanac was published during the period . . ."[90]

The following was another typical advertisement of some current literature for sale at the book store and was quite characteristic of the standards of the time:

The Young Gentlemen's and Lady's
MONITOR
and English Teacher's Assistant
Being Collections of Select Pieces from
Our Best MODERN WRITERS,
Calculated to Eradicate Vulgar
Prejudices and Rusticity of Manners
Improve the Understanding; Rectify the Will,
Purify the Passions, Direct the Minds of
Youth to the Pursuit of Proper Objects, and
facilitate their Reading, Writing and
Speaking the English Language
with Elegance and Propriety.[91]

There was an interesting advertisement in the April 12, 1792 issue of the *Herald* which may or may not have been usual for that period. Whether this advertisement succeeded in its purpose is in doubt. There are no records of anyone having seen this book, and there are no copies of it extant.

Proposal for Printing . . .
The Poor Man's Help and Young Man's Guide by
William Burkett, M. A.
Conditions

I. The work shall be printed on a good paper and a large fair type.
II. They shall be delivered either in a plain or in a neat binding, as the subscriber chuses.
III. It will contain about 200 pp. in large Octavo
IV. The price to Subscribers will be 3 shillings and sixpence plain binding, and 4 shillings and 6 pence Gilt and Lettered.

V. Those who subscribe and pay for a dozen will be entitled to one gratis.

VI. No money will be exacted, until the Books are delivered, and then it is expected punctual payment will be made.

VII. As soon as 400 subscribers are obtained the work will be put to press and finished with all expedition.

Therefore, the Author of this valuable book is so well known, that all encomiums will be needless . Suffice it is to say that this book for its excellency has within these 2 years ran thro' 2 large editions in the City of New York.

Subscriptions are now taken in at this Office but subscrip-scription papers will be issued, and left at most public offices on the island.[92]

That Frothingham was operating a stationery store with a large assortment of materials to provide the area with a degree of culture, and mental and moral advancement, can be gleaned from this advertisement:

Books

Just received to be sold at Printing Office, the following Books.

Sterne's Works—5 vol.

Guthrie's Grammar, late edition

Pope's Works complete

Christian's, Scholar's and Farmer's Magazines

The Messiah, by the author of the Death of Abel

Watts' Psalms revised by Barkow, good print

Sermons for Children, by Samuel Spring

Holiday Exercises or the Christian ABC

Delworth Spelling Book, &c.

A great variety of Children's Books among which are Dr. Watts' Divine Songs, the Picture Alphabet, a book well calculated to learn Children their letters.

A very fine Assortment of colored PICTURES

Writing Paper, very good, per quire

Wrapping Paper by the Ream &c.

Wafers &c, &c

Any of the above articles can be exchanged for Clean Cotton or Linnen Raggs[93]

David Frothingham professed an interest in improving the mind by presenting the best in literature. A study of the literary material printed in the *Herald* may indicate the standards for the "best in literature" of the reading public at that time. Not only was the language of such literature flowery and highly complex, but when the subject was not dedicated to the purpose of improving the morals, it seemed to dwell heavily toward the general category of "Vice" with its "concomitant attendants." An excerpt, taken at random from a column length story might help to illustrate the style, quality, and subject matter of the literary contributions of the *Herald*:

As he was staggering home one night from a party with some of his libertine companions, he was accosted by a female, who had something in her air and manner so different from those outcasts of humanity who offer themselves to casual prostitution in the streets that his curiosity was aroused . . . He viewed her with a silent compassion for some moments and reaching for a piece of gold, bade her go home and shelter herself from the inclemency of the weather at so late an hour. Her surprise and joy at such unexpected charity overpowered her, . . . [94]

Short news items drawn from different parts of the world seemed to dwell on the subjects of scandal, seduction, and murder, with all the gory details included. Each issue contained more than one of these juicy, spicy morsels for the edification of its readers. Considering the strict Puritan moral code of the period, with its strong emphasis on

Virtue, and the popularity of the printed sermons it is surprising that material of such questionable taste should abound side by side with items on Chastity, and the like.

Included in the regular format of the *Long Island Herald* were the Anecdotes many of which featured the *double entendre* that would certainly never be allowed to pass the most broadminded newspaper censorship today. It is difficult to correlate straightlaced descendants from Puritan New England, on the one hand, and public exposure to such risque "literature" on the other.

That these little "Anecdotes" were of an indelicate nature and were possibly an attempt to inject a suggestion of light humor into an otherwise serious journal once again illustrates the flavor of the reading taste of the period. The first reaction might be that Frothingham was contradicting his own editorial policy, but the apparent acceptance of such material by the subscribers serves to illustrate a difference between the culture of Colonial Long Island and that of the present day.

Frothingham's Long Island Herald followed the pattern of other country newspapers of that era. Prior to the day of the reporter or of rapid communications, its contents were mostly reprints from week-old or month-old city newspapers, republished public documents, and legislative records. With the exception of some signed announcements by him, which were usually printed on the third column of the third page, Frothingham's name did not appear elsewhere in the paper. As was the custom of the time, contributions that were printed and signed usually had names as Juno, or Brutus, or the Observer, or the Moralist, etc. It would be assumed that his own tastes and sentiments determined what selections were to be included in his paper.

The question arises, did David Frothingham, as printer, publisher, and editor of his paper decide what was to be printed in his paper? During the course of this study it has become increasingly clear that control of the contents of the paper was not entirely in his own hands. In order to trace the answer to this question, it is necessary to go back to the beginning when David Frothingham first came to Sag Harbor.

There are several ways in which an establishment of a pioneer press was undertaken. First, an enterprising printer might invade virgin territory and appealing to the inhabitants insure himself enough support to launch his paper. A second method was that in which the initiative came from a group in the community who sought out and financed a printer. A third method similar to the second, was to secure support for the printer from a single patron.[95]

In the early issues of the *Herald*, one of the contributors was the *Philanthropist* whose column of considerable length appeared on the front

page. A casual glance at the column would sug-
gest that it followed Frothingham's promise of
damning Vice and was "consistent with the rigid
line of Virtue." [96] An excerpt from the column of
June 21, 1791, when the paper was about six
weeks old, will illustrate the style and nature of
the contents of the column:

... The flaming patriot pitties the servile condition of the subject of the despot, who is incumbered with the shackles of slavery, whilst on the other hand the republican is held to be a fit
subject of comiseration as dwelling under a government, void
of energy, subject of the instability, anarchy, and confusion,
and whilst the subject of the despot beholds the irregularities of
the republican government, he glories in his own, as opposed to
it, and places the summit of virtue in being loyal to one who is
riviting the chains of slavery fast upon him. [97]

The story of the *Philanthropist* provides insight
into the manner by which material was included
in the *Herald*. Stephen Burroughs, whose *Memoirs*
describe unashamedly a life of scorn for all de-
cencies of law and order, had fled to Shelter Island
under the alias of Stephen Edenson and stayed
at an inn owned by "Uncle Jim" Havens. "Uncle
Jim" was very friendly with Judge Havens, Mr.
Nichols, Colonel Dearing, and others who came
and visited at the inn very often. Burroughs' com-
ments, written "with sophisticated wickedness,
that kind that knows its ground and can twin-
kle" [98] are of some note. Judge Havens appeared
as "a man of unshaken integrity, much attached

to order and regularity as a member of society,* Mr. Nichols was rich, and Colonel Dearing owned a large estate, was extremely haughty and was a "Presbyterian bigot."[100] As for the people, Burroughs had this to say:

"People on this island were very illiterate, making but a small calculation for information further than the narrow circle of their business extended. They were almost entirely destitute of books of any kind, except school books and Bibles; hence those who had a taste for reading, had not the opportunity."[101]

As Burroughs continued his stay at the inn, he became better acquainted with "Uncle Jim" who eventually wormed out of Burroughs his true identity and his reason for being on the Island. One day, the innkeeper suggested to Burroughs "the idea of writing for the periodical publication of the press. This subject did not find an agreeable place in my mind. I was a stranger in the place; I was ignorant of the pre-

---

*Burroughs probably had reference to Jonathan N. Havens, later a member of Congress, whose Obituary appeared in *Greenleaf's New York Journal and Patriotic Register*, November 2, 1799: "We condole with the constituents of this honest respectable Representative, upon the loss which they have sustained by his decease. Faithfully did he discharge his duties of his station; interested views never induced him to deviate for a moment from the principles of a Republican; nor could the arts or address of sophists deceive his penetration. His private was no less amiable than his public character; benificence and philanthrophy were his characteristics. In the happiness of others, he found the greatest pleasure and he was ever ready to soothe and console the poor, the afflicted or the unfortunate. Alas, he is no more."[99]

valent ideas of the country, their political and moral character."[102] The innkeeper persisted, suggesting secrecy.

I began my literary task under the name of the Philanthropist. I had proceeded as far as the fourth or fifth number before anything of note took place in consequence of these publications. . . At length, a clergyman of Southampton* taking alarm of some sentiments here manifested, Published a very spirited answer to them.† A reply on my part was then avoidable. The clergy answered by reply, and I rejoined with an answer. By this time the attention of the public was excited to the controversy, more than to the merit of the publications, and they were anxious to know the combatants. It was known at the printing office that Uncle Jim uniformly brought the Philanthropist for publication; and also that the manuscripts were ever in his handwriting. These circumstances turned the eyes of the public upon him, and he possessed the fortitude for some time, to retain the secret but at length it became a burden for him to support alone.

Therefore, he imparted it to some of his intimate friends who compassionately relieved him from the cumber, by dissolving the charm of secrecy and giving the matter to the public.

I now found a retreat the only place of safety, and therefore withdrew my lucubrations from the press, and here ended the matter, as it related to me in the character of The Philanthropist.[105]

An ironic postscript to this fiasco of *The Philanthropist* was an item in the December 17, 1798, issue of the *Herald*, the last known edition printed under the direction of David Frothingham.

---

*Mr. Daggett.[103]

†Excerpt of a letter sent by Mr. Daggett dated November 14, 1791: . . . To the public he appeared in the double capacity of the Philanthropist calling all mankind to 'cooperate with him,' in the establishment of universal benevolence, on the ruins of superstition; and of an Observer, to support his works against the rude assault of criticism.[104]

Quere — Would not a work with the following title be as popular as the MORAL memoirs of Burroughs? A history of the
Devil written by himself at the request of many of his readers.[106]

This account of Stephen Burroughs, as one of
the contributors to the *Herald*, seems to indicate
carte blanche acceptance by Frothingham of material given to him by certain people. How many
times this was repeated through the years can
only be surmised.

The number of copies printed of each issue of
the *Herald* is not known. But it must be borne in
mind that the weekly output would not be any indication of the true circulation of the newspaper.
With the scarcity of reading material in most
homes, perhaps nothing more than a Bible or possibly an almanac, the weekly newspaper with its
news of the outside world was read and re-read
from the top of the first page to the last column
of the last page, including advertisements and
notices, laws and speeches. Most likely it was
handed from one person to another, from one
family to another. Country people were fortu-
nate indeed if there was a press nearby. Rarely
did they have the opportunity to read any other
but the local newspaper. After a while, the readers
absorbed the philosophy of the local printer and
his newspaper. In this way did the country
printer mold public opinion.

Frothingham's Long Island Herald, printed
at Sag Harbor on the east end of Long Island, but

circulated throughout the Island and in New York City as well was one of many country presses in New York State. As an individual press following the pattern of systematic Republican persuasion, perhaps its influence may have been slight, but joined with the other Republican presses who used similar journalistic tactics, it became powerful enough to effect a reaction that resulted in the passing of the Alien and Sedition Laws in an effort to smother the power of the press.

David Lord of Morristown, New Jersey, sent the following letter to Alexander Hamilton on April 11, 1798:

. . . The greatest evil that pervades our country is the country press. These have been, many of them, set up and supported by the Democratic party in different places, and those not actually raised by their private collections of money have been as it were seized or hired by the party to retail scandal against the government so that 9/10ths of the Presses out of the great towns in America south of the Hudson are Democratic and most of them by direct pay or influence. While the opposers of the government are doing all this and ten times as much by misrepresentations, the wealth, information, and abilities of our country are not excited at all or very little indeed.[107]

EVALUATION

DAVID FROTHINGHAM has an indisputable claim to fame. He was the first printer of the first press on Long Island; his newspaper *Frothingham's Long Island Herald* was the first newspaper published on Long Island; his *Long Island Magazine* was the first magazine published on Long Island; and the books from his press were the first books published on Long Island. Yet, neither his press, his newspaper, his magazine, nor his books were successful. His life, of which thirty-five years could be accounted for, would be considered a failure.

Born during a period and in a place of political crisis, his younger years were further disturbed by the loss of his father and his stepfather. Hostilities with England took place almost as close as his back yard. During the years before the actual outbreak of war, rebellion was brewing in and around Charlestown. If he had any feeling of security, it might well have been undermined by the growing discontent and excitement that surrounded him. He lived in the immediate vicinity of the Revolution and saw the occupation of Boston by the British. The atmosphere of hostility and rebellion against the Brit-

ish, in which he was probably bred during his
early youth, remained with him in his adult years
and was given expression through his newspaper
at Sag Harbor. Penniless when he married
Nancy Pell, who had been disowned by her
father, and already saddled with a family, he
came to New York. His choice of Sag Harbor
and his negotiations with Henry Dering must
have appealed to him as the big opportunity for
fame and fortune. He received neither there.

Being chosen by the famous Aaron Burr (at
this time Burr was still not notorious) to act as
his sounding board on a New York newspaper at
eight dollars per week must have appeared to him
once more as the big opportunity, It was an
honor to be recognized by a great leader and to
serve the Republican cause in a larger sphere.
That opportunity ended in failure and disgrace.
As far as can be determined, it also ended in obli-
vion. He disappeared, leaving a wife and six
children in Sag Harbor, as well as a mortgage on
his press.

Nothing is known about his appearance, his
personality, his education, his training period as
an apprentice printer, or about his life with Nancy Pell. Though the information on David Frothingham is scanty, and a conclusion can be drawn
from a cursory examination of known data that
he failed in every venture, a closer analysis of

what material is available might just as readily lead to another conclusion.

When all factors of the times are considered, David Frothingham becomes a mirror that reflects a most crucial period in American history. His campaign against England, his contempt for the Federalists and their emulation of the English, his pleas for friendship with France, his alignment on the side of the Republicans in the hope that their policies would be the means of saving our liberties at home and our dignity abroad, all succeeded after his disappearance. Though he was sacrificed under the knife of the Alien and Sedition Laws, that sacrifice helped in the defeat of the Federalists in New York and in the election of 1800. His trial highlighted the evils of the Federalist Alien and Sedition Laws. It brought home to the readers of the New York journals the fear of the endangerment of their liberties. His trial was a result of a law enacted by the Federalist government in desperation at an inability to halt the continuous pounding and criticism of the Republican press.

David Frothingham's *Long Island Herald* was a country newspaper typical of those published in the last decade of the eighteenth century. A study of its pages with their unclear print, archaic inconsistent spelling, conglomeration of substandard literary forms, its stale news excerpts clipped according to the whim of the Editor or another* who might have been in control of the press, its verbatim legal and legislative announcements, and its oftimes questionable taste, comes as quite a shock at first to a reader who is accustomed to the accepted standards of modern journalism.

However, the fact that the newspaper was distributed and read by hundreds of people week after week over a period of many years would indicate that it cannot be dismissed as inconsequential.

In his discussion of the unprincipled ruthlessness of these newspapers, Lee states in defense of the Federalists for the enactment of the Alien and Sedition Laws:

That the American press from 1790 to 1800 was probably as powerful in its influence as at any time in its history is not to be denied. But the violence and vituperation of the party press had to result in the first attempt of the American government to regulate the newspaper press. The year of 1798 saw the passage of the Alien and Sedition Laws.[109]

Milton Hamilton, in his discussion of this subject, has this comment in rebuttal:

Not to have permitted free criticism would have been to sacrafice the most valuable fruits of national experience. Political and ethical codes were in the process of formation. Not to have per-

---

*"A man of some means who had investments in the new country, who was interested in politics or who was the principal citizen in a growing community, might employ a printer and provide an establishment to serve his purposes."[108] The prinpal patron of the press in Sag Harbor was Henry Dering, Collector of the Port.

mitted free criticism of public servants would have led to the sanction of evil practices. Printers and editors may not have been individually powerful, but collectively, they were a power. While blaming or pitying the printers for their lapses and their incapacity, we would warmly commend them for a courageous exercise of freedom of expression.[110]

It is to be noted in the preceding paragraph that "they may not have been individually powerful, but collectively they were a power." *Frothingham's Long Island Herald* evidently was sufficiently "powerful" to attract the attention of Aaron Burr and inspire him with the confidence to entrust Frothingham with the responsibility of promoting public opinion in favor of the Republicans in the big city of New York.

At the time that *Frothingham's Long Island Herald* ended and Frothingham's employment on the *Argus* began, when the eighteenth century was drawing to a close, the wheels of politics were grinding rapidly to a dramatic climax. The attacks by the various Republican presses continued unchecked by the Alien and Sedition Laws. Aaron Burr and his political acumen in Albany effected the formation of a competitive bank in New York City that dissolved the monopoly of Alexander Hamilton and the Federalists. The presidential campaign, prior to the election of 1800, was in progress, and the Federalist control of the government was in jeopardy. These factors contributed to upset the composure of Alexander Hamilton and caused him to institute his libel suit against David Frothingham.

Was Alexander Hamilton really after David Frothingham's scalp. It is to be doubted, Frothingham merely represented "The Enemy" to him. "The Enemy" could have been Burr, Jefferson, Republicans, newspapers, printers, anybody or anything that criticized the Federalist government in general or Alexander Hamilton in particular.

The study of the first newspaper press at Sag Harbor and its printer has revealed interesting sidelights on several famous personalities of the Colonial period. It becomes increasingly evident that these political figures at the inception of the new nation were hungry for power and control according to their individual ideals. Quite often words and deeds did not seem to correspond. The terms Federalist, Anti-Federalist, Republican and Democrat did not represent the same thing to all people. Aaron Burr and Thomas Jefferson, though both Republicans, did not advocate the same principles. They were alike in that they were both against the Federalists. Nor does Washington emerge as the great political leader of the Federalists that he is reputed to have been while he was President. Alexander Hamilton seemed to be the power behind the scenes, a snob, ambitious for personal glory, and not always ethical or consistent in his methods.

The case of Frothingham's libel was a farce of political justice. The sparring between the defense attorney, Brockholst Livingston, close ally of Aaron Burr, and Alexander Hamilton was another opportunity for both to resort to political invective.

Ironically enough, Alexander Hamilton, acting as defense attorney for the printer, Croswell, in a libel suit several years later, made the following statement on behalf of his client:

The Liberty of the Press consists of the right to publish with Impunity — Truth with good motives for justifiable Ends, though reflecting on Government, Magistracy, or Individuals.[111]

Historically the libel trial of Frothingham is not recorded as a battle between Aaron Burr and Alexander Hamilton, though this, in fact, is what it was.   Hamilton, in attempting to stifle the stinging Republican press, was seeking revenge on Burr for a long list of past grievances. No doubt, the bitterness generated at the trial was another of the seeds of hatred planted between Hamilton and Burr that was later to erupt so disastrously.

In 1800, the Federalists lost the election in New York City. They were defeated on Long Island. The long and deliberate campaign of Anti-Federalist journalist hysteria had succeeded in ousting the Federalists from power at last. The election resulted in a tie vote between Aaron Burr and Thomas Jefferson for President of the

United States. It was through the efforts of Alexander Hamilton that the tie was broken in favor of Thomas Jefferson. With the retirement of the Federalists from power came the end of the Alien and Sedition Laws as well.

The events of the early years of the United States were all recorded in the pages of *Frothingham's Long Island Herald* a week or a month after they occurred. The "impartial" editorial policy of its printer reveals the growing pains of the new nation and the struggle for power and principles among its political leaders during America's first decade as an independent nation.

CITATIONS

1. Charles A. Beard, *Economic Origins of Jeffersonian Democracy*, p. 4.

2. Samuel H. Wandell and Meade Minnigerode, *Aaron Burr*, Vol. I, p. 28.

3. *Loc. cit.*

4. Harry D. Sleight, *Sag Harbor in the Earlier Days*, p. 69.

5. Milton W. Hamilton, *The Country Printer, 1785-1830*, "Foreword" by Dixon Ryan Fox, n. p.

6. Letter from Selleck Osborn to Henry P. Dering, December 9, 1801, MS in Morton Pennypacker Long Island Collection, Easthampton Free Library, Easthampton, N.Y., No. KR23.

7. Louis Tooker Vail, "David Frothingham, First Printer of Long Island; A Martyr to the Freedom of the Press," preface n. p., MS in the Morton Pennypacker Long Island Collection, Easthampton Free Library, Easthampton, N. Y., No. 8526.

8. Richard Frothingham, Jr., *The History of Charlestowne Mass.*, p. 280.

9. *Loc. cit.*

10. Frothingham, op. cit., p. 281.

11. *Ibid.*, p. 280.

12. *Ibid.*, p. 282.

13. *Ibid.*, p. 290.

14. Benjamin F. Thompson, *History of Long Island*, vol. 2, p. 224.

15. Letter from Selleck Osborn to Henry P. Dering, December 9, 1801, MS in Morton Pennypacker Long Island Collection, Easthampton Free Library, Easthampton, N. Y., No. KR23.

16. Letter from David Gardiner, Jr. to Henry P. Dering, January 25, 1791, MS in Morton Pennypacker Long Island Collection, Easthampton Free Library, Easthampton, N. Y., No. KR23.

17. Letter from David Frothingham to Henry P. Dering, February 7, 1791, MS in Morton Pennypacker Long Island Collection, Easthampton Free Library, Easthampton, N. Y., No. KR23.

18. *Frothingham's Long Island Herald*, Sag Harbor, N. Y., May 10, 1791, p. 1.

19. *Loc. cit.*

20. William S. Pelletreau, *History of Long Island*, Vol. II, p. 505.

21. *Herald*, June 14, 1791, p. 3.

22. Hamilton, *op. cit.*, p. 216.

23. *Herald*, June 21, 1791, p. 3.

24. *Ibid*, October 30, 1797, p. 3.

25. Hamilton, *op. cit.*, p. 10.

26. *Herald*, August 23, 1791, p. 3.

27. *Ibid.*, May 3, 1793, p. 3.

28. *Ibid.*, June 21, 1797, p. 4.

29. *Ibid.*, October 18, 1797, p. 3.

30. *Ibid.*, October 18, 1797, p. 3.

31. Hamilton, *op. cit.*, p. 170.

32. Clarence S. Brigham, *History and Bibliography of American Newspapers, 1690-1820*, Vol.I, p. 730.

33. Letter from Selleck Osborne to Henry P. Dering, February 21, 1802, MS in Morton Pennypacker Long Island Collection, Easthampton Free Library, Easthampton, N. Y., No, KR23.

34. *Herald*, July 9, 1798, p. 3.

35. *Ibid.*, June 7, 1791, p. 3.

36. Jacqueline Overton, *Long Island's Story*, p. 186.

37. Pelletreau, *op. cit.*, p. 511.

38. William Wallace Tooker, *David Frothingham, an Early Sag Harbor Printer*, n. p.

39. *Herald*, July 23, 1798, p. 3.

40. *Ibid.*, August 13, 1798, p. 4.

41. *Greenleaf's New York Journal and Patriotic Register*, December 22, 1798, p. 3.

42. *Ibid.*, December 11, 1799, p. 1.

43. *Hamilton*, op.cit., p. 174.

44. Wandell and Minnigerode, *op. cit.*, p. 177.

45. Henry Cabot Lodge, *Alexander Hamilton*, p 260.

46. *Greenleaf's New York Journal and Patriotic Register*, December 11, 1799, pp. 1-2.

47. Wandell and Minnigerode, *op. cit.*, p. 177.

48. *Greenleaf's New York Journal and Patriotic Register*, November,13, 1799, p. 3.

49. *Loc. cit.*

50. *Greenleaf's New York Journal and Patriotic Register*, November 20, 1799, p. 3.

51. *Ibid.*, December 7, 1799, p. 4.

52. *Ibid.*, December 11, 1799, p. 1.

53. *Loc. cit..*

54. *Loc. cit.*

55. *Loc. cit.*

56. Vail, *op. cit.*, n. p.

57. *Greenleaf's New York Journal and Patriotic Register*, December 7, 1799, p. 3.

58. Letter from Paul E. Lockwood, Executive Assistant to District Attorney Thomas E. Dewey, to Louis Tooker Vail, August 18, 1939, quoted in Vail, *op. cit.*, n. p.

59. *Greenleaf's New York Journal and Patriotic Register*, December 25, 1799, p. 3.

60. *Herald*, May 10, 1791, p. 1.

61. *Ibid.*, September 20, 1797, p. 1.

62. *Ibid.*, July 23, 1798, p. 3.

63. *Ibid.*, September 20, 1797, p. 3.

64. *Ibid.*, April 19, 1797, p. 4.

65. *Ibid.*, May 24, 1797, p. 1.

66. *Ibid.*, May 31, 1797, p. 1.

67. *Ibid.*, June 21, p. 1.

68. *Ibid.*, June 21, p. 3

69. *Ibid.*, June 28, 1797, p. 1.

70. *Ibid.*, September 20, 1797, p. 4.

71. *Ibid.*, April 12, 1797, p 3.

72 Mortgage between David Frothingham and Henry P. Dering, et. al., February 1, 1797, MS in Morton Pennypacker Long Island Collection, Easthampton Free Library, Easthampton, New York, No. KR23.

73. *Herald*, August 9, 1797, p. 3.

74. *Ibid.*, June 25, 1798, p. 3.

75. *Loc. cit.*

76. *Herald*, September 27, 1797, p.3.

77. *Ibid.*, September 13, 1797, p. 3.

78. *Loc. cit.*

79. *Herald*, May 10, 1797, p. 4.

80. *Loc. cit.*

81. *Loc. cit.*

82. *Loc cit.*

83. *Herald*, June 21, 1797, p. 4.

84. *Ibid.*, May 10, 1797, p.4.

85. *Ibid.* March 1797, p. 4.

86. *Ibid.*, August 9, 1791, p. 3.

87. *Ibid.*, August 30, 1791, p. 3.

88. *Ibid.*, June 7, 1791, p. 3.

89. *Ibid.*, December 13, 1791, p. 4.

90. Douglas C. McMurtrie, *American Imprints: A Check List of the Imprints of Sag Harbor*, preface, p. xv.

91. *Herald*, December 13, 1791, p. 4.

92. *Ibid.*, April 12, 1792, p. 3.

93. *Ibid.*, June 21, 1791, p. 3.

94. *Ibid.*, May 24, 1797, p. 4.

95. Hamilton, *op. cit.*, p. 51.

96. *Herald*, June 14, 1791, p. 1.

97. *Ibid.*, June 21, 1791, p. 1.

98. Stephen Burroughs, *Memoirs of the Notorious Stephen Burroughs of New Hampshire*, ed., by Lincoln MacVeigh, "Preface" by Robert Frost, p. vi.

99. *Greenleaf's New York Journal and Patriotic Register*, November 2, 1799, p. 3.

100. Burroughs, *Memoirs of the Notorious Stephen Burroughs of New Hampshire*, p. 248.

101. *Ibid.*, p. 279.

102. *Ibid.*, p. 254.

103. *Ibid.*, p. 277

104. *Ibid.*, p. 274.

105. *Ibid.*, pp. 254-255.

106. *Herald*, December 17, 1798, p. 3.

107. Beard, op. cit., p. 196.

108. John E. Winterich, *Early American Books and Printing*, p. 54.

109. James Melvin Lee, *op. cit.*, p. 102.

110. Hamilton, *op. cit.*, p. 207.

111. *Ibid.*, p. 172.

BIBLIOGRAPHY

Primary Sources

Documents

Mortgage agreement between David Frothingham and Henry P. Dering, John N. Fordham, and Jessie Hodges. February 1, 1797. MS in Morton Pennypacker Long Island Collection, Easthampton Free Library, Easthampton, N. Y., No. KR23.

Letters

David Gardiner, Jr. to Henry P. Dering, January 25, 1791. MS in Morton Pennypacker Long Island Collection, Easthampton Free Library, Easthampton, N. Y., No.KR23.

David Frothingham to Henry P. Dering. February 7, 1791. MS in Morton Pennypacker Long Island Collection, Easthampton Free Library, Easthampton, N. Y., No. KR23.

Selleck Osborn to Henry P. Dering, December 9, 1801. MS in Morton Pennypacker Long Island Collection, Easthampton Free Library, Easthampton, N. Y., No. KR23.

Selleck Osborn to Henry P. Dering. February 21, 1802. MS in Morton Pennypacker Long Island Collection, Easthampton Free Library, Easthampton, N. Y., No. KR23.

Newspapers

Frothingham's Long Island Herald. Sag Harbor, N. Y.:
All issues from May 10, 1791 through December 17, 1798.

Greenleaf's New York Journal and Patriotic Register New York:
December 22, 1798; November 2, 13, 20, 1799; December 7. 11, 14. 25, 1799.

Secondary Sources

Adams, James Truslow. *History of the Town of Southampton* (East of Canoe Place). Bridgehampton: Hampton Press, 1918. (Reprint Edition, Port Washington, N. Y. Ira J. Friedman Inc. 1962)

American Heritage. *Thomas Jefferson and His World,* by the editors of *American Heritage,* narrative by Henry Moscow and Douglas Malone. New York: American Heritage Publishing Co., Inc., 1960.

Beard, Charles A. *Economic Origins of Jeffersonian Democracy.* New York: The Macmillan Co., 1949.

Brigham, Clarence S. *History and Bibliography of American Newspapers. 1690-1820.* Worcester: American Antiquarian Society, 1947.

Brooklyn Daily Eagle. October 28, 1934. Mounted Clipping in Long Island Collection, Queensborough Public Library, Jamaica, N. Y., "Sag Harbor" folder.

Brooklyn Times Union. July 3, 1932. Mounted Clipping in Long Island Collection, Queensborough Public Library, Jamaica, N. Y., "Sag Harbor" folder.

Burroughs, Stephen. *Memoirs of the Notorious Stephen Burroughs of New Hampshire,* ed. by Lincoln MacVeigh. New York: Dial Press, 1924.

Crouse, Anna Erskine and Crouse, Russell. *Alexander Hamilton and Aaron Burr; Their Lives, Their Times, Their Duel.* New York: Random House, 1958.

D'Emo, Beatrice. "Editor of First Long Island Paper Libeled Hamilton and Went to Jail." *Forest Hills-Kew Gardens Post,* August 7, 1930, p.1.

Duvall, Ralph G. *History of Shelter Island: From Its Settlement in 1652 to the Present Time, 1932.* Shelter Island Heights.: by the author, 1932.

Flint, Martha B. *Early Long Island; Colonial Study.* New York: Putnam's Sons, 1896.

Frothingham, Richard Jr.*History of Charlestowne, Mass.* Boston: Charles C. Little and James Brown, 1845.

Hamilton, Milton W. *The Country Printer, 1785-1830,* ed. by Dixon Ryan Fox. ("New York State Historical Series," Vol. IV). New York: Columbia University Press, 1936 (Reprint Edition, Port Washington, N. Y. Ira J. Friedman, 1963.)

Hazelton, Henry Isham. *Boroughs of Brooklyn and Queens, Counties of Nassau and Suffolk, Long Island, New York 1924.* New York and Chicago: Lewis Publishing Co., Inc., 1925

History of Suffolk County; Comprising the Addresses at the Cele-bration of the Bi-Centennial of Suffolk County, N. Y., in Ri-verhead, November 15, 1883. Babylon: Budget Steam Print, 1885.

Judson, Clara Ingram.   *Thomas Jefferson, Champion of the People,* Chicago: Follet Publishing Co., 1952.

Lee, James Melvin.   *History of American Journalism.* Revised edition. Garden City: Garden City Publishing Co., Inc., 1923.

Lehman-Haupt, Helmut; Wroth Lawrence, and Silver, Rollo G. *The Book in America; A History of the Making and Selling of Books in the United States.* 2nd. edition. New York: R. R. Bowker, 1951

Lewis, Arnold Meredith.   "Sag Harbor; A Study of a Small Com-munity." Unpublished Master's thesis, Young Men's Chris-tian Association College, Springfield, Mass., June 15, 1931. MS in Morton Pennypacker Long Island Collection, East-hampton Free Library, Easthampton, N. Y., No. JD57.

Lodge, Henry Cabot. *Alexander Hamilton. ("American Statesmen Series,"* Vol. VII).   Boston; Houghton, 1899.

McMurtrie, Douglas C.   *American Imprints; A check List of the Imprints of Sag Harbor,L.I- 1791-1820.* ("American Imprints Inventory, " Vol. XII, The WPA Historical Records Survey Program, Division of Professional and Service Project Ad-ministration). Chicago: The WPA Historic Records Survey Project, 1939.

One Hundredth Anniversary, 1860-1960; One Hundred Years with the Sag Harbor Savings Bank--A century of Progress. Sag Harbor: Sag Harbor Savings Bank, 1960.

Overton, Jacqueline. *Long Island's Story.* Garden City:Double-day, Doran, and Co., 1929 (Second Edition Port Washing-ton, N. Y., I. J. Friedman, Inc.1961).

Pelletreau, William S.   *History of Long Island; From its Earliest Settlement to the Present Time.* New York and Chicago: Lewis Publishing Co., 1903.

Pennypacker, Morton.   "Bank of Manhattan Company Owes its Existence to a Long Island Printer."   *Brooklyn Daily Eagle,* September 19, 1928. Clipping in Long Island Histor-ical Society, Brooklyn, N. Y., *"Frothingham's Long Island Herald"* folder.

——————. *General Washington's Spies on Long Island and in New York*. Brooklyn: Long Island Historical Society, 1939.

——————. *Long Island's First Printer's Devil*. Kew Gardens, By the author, 1927.

——————. "Biographical Sketch of David Frothingham." MS in Morton Pennypacker Long Island Collection, Easthampton Free Library, Easthampton, N. Y., No. RF 260.

Ross, Peter. *History of Long Island; From its Earliest Settlement to the Present Time*. Vol. I. New York and Chicago: Lewis Publishing Co., 1903.

Sealock, Richard P. and Seely, Pauline A. *Long Island Bibliography*. Baltimore; 1949.

Scudder, Henry J. "Formation of the Civil Government of Suffolk County." in *History of Suffolk County: Comprising the Addresses at the Celebration of the Bi-Centennial of Suffolk County, N. Y., in Riverhead, November 15, 1883*. Babylon : Budget Steam Print, 1885.

Sleight, Harry D. *Sag Harbor in the Earlier Days; A Series of Historical Sketches of the Harbor and Hampton Port*. Sag Harbor: By the author, 1930.

——————.*Sleights of Sag Harbor*. Bridgehampton: By the author, 1929.

Thompson, Benjamin F. From its Discovery and Settlement to the Present Time. 3rd Edition, Revised and greatly enlarged with a biography of the author by Charles J, Werner. Three Volumes, New York, William H. Dodd. 1918 (Reprint Edition Port Washington, N. Y. I. J. Friedman, Inc. 1962).

Tooker, William Wallace. "David Frothingham, an Early Sag Harbor Printer." Paper read before the meeting of the Sag Harbor Historical Society, Sag Harbor, N. Y., N. Y., January 2, 1902.

Vail, Louis Tooker. "David Frothingham, First Printer of Long Island; A Martyr to the Freedom of the Press." Unpublished MS in Morton Pennypacker Long Island Collection, Easthampton Public Library, Easthampton, N. Y., RF260

Waldman, Milton. *Americana; The Literature of American History*. New York: Henry Holt and Co., 1923.

Wandell, Samuel Henry, and Minnigerode Meade. *Aaron Burr A Biography, Written in Large Part from Original and Hitherto Unused Material*. New York: G. P. Putnam's Sons, 1925.

Whitaker, Epher. "Growth of Suffolk County in Population, Wealth, and Comfort," in *History of Suffolk County ;Compprising the Addresses at the Celebration of the Bi-Centennial of Suffolk County, N. Y.. in Riverhead, November 15, 1883.*

Willey, Nancy Boyd. *Built by the Whalers; A tour of Historic Sag Harbor and its Colonial Archicteture.* Sag Harbor: By the Author, 1945. (3rd edition published by the Old Sagg-Harbor Committee, 1951).

—————. *Story of Sag Harbor, L. I.* Sag Harbor: Herald House, 1945.

—————. *David Frothingham, Pioneer Editor.* Bay Shore: Long Island Forum. 1941.

—————. "Herald House, Sag Harbor," *Long Island Forum,* III. (May, 1940), pp. 95-96.

Wyman, Thomas Bellows. *Genealogies and Estates of Charlestown in the County of Middlesex and Commonwealth of Massachusetts, 1629-1818.* 2 vols. Boston: David Cladd and Sons, 1879.

Winterich, John T. *Early American Books and Printing* Boston: Houghton, Mifflin Company, **1935**.

INDEX

Frothingham's Lo

EYE NATURE'S WALKS, SHOOT FOLLY AS IT FLIES

No. I.]   T U E S D .

To THE *PUBLIC*.

WITH the greateſt deference the firſt Number of the HERALD is laid before the
Public, on whoſe ſmiles the Editor founds his
hope of patronage, and expects ſo laudable an
undertaking will meet with encouragement tantamount to its merits. Too much puffing is
frequently, on this occaſion, made uſe of by
publiſhers ; but when the Editor ſhall ceaſe to
merit applauſe, he will no longer wiſh the favor
of the public extended to him. Neither diligence
nor labor ſhall be wanting to render this paper
a uſeful repoſitory of knowledge, humour, and
entertainment ; while Vice, the bane of ſociety,
with its concomitant attendants, though cloathed
with the garb of authority, will be branded with
every mark of infamy.

Whatever has a tendency to expand the mind,
and embeliſh the underſtanding, will be proſecuted
with infatigable zeal ; and every branch of
literature ranſacked to enlighten and enlarge the
faculties of the human mind. In a word we
ſhall

"" Eye nature's walks, ſhoot folly as it flies,
"" And catch the manners living as they riſe.""

In the courſe of this publication, a corner will
be devoted to the treaſure of thoſe in the Poetic
line, whoſe correſpondence, together with thoſe
in the Proſaic walk, are earneſtly requeſted.

DAVID FROTHINGHAM.

robbery." " Well, bu
" had you no fear of
the fellow, looking
is that to you, if I ha
You had removed my
I fear the leaſt ?"

To Prevent UN
Thoughts ſubmitted
vention of
1. Let every man
enough to be his g
ideot ; and let the ne
cent or imitation, in
2. When two old,
enter into the bands
ed non compos, and
3. When a fine yo
health and gaiety, m
widow, let it be adm
be acquitted accordi
4. Let the lady be
be lucky enough to
mand reſtitution of
5. When a woman
ingly a ſpendthrift, le
and loſe her pariſh.
6. When a man or
ſion or injury of thei
be found guilty of
death accordingly.
7. When a man n
ſtudy patience from
a ſtring of magpies
life.
8. When a giddy b
without profeſſion,
let them be immediat
of no other uſe in ſ
gation.
9. When a gentlem
maid, and when a
ſtable-boy, let the